JAMES SI

THE
EXPERIENCE
BUSINESS

Why Price-Focused Businesses Fail
and What Winners Do Instead

First published in Great Britain 2017 by Rethink
Press (www.rethinkpress.com)

© Copyright James Sinclair

All rights reserved. No part of this publication may be reproduced, stored
in or introduced into a retrieval system, or transmitted, in any form, or
by any means (electronic, mechanical, photocopying, recording or
otherwise) without the prior written permission of the publisher.

The right of James Sinclair to be identified as the author of
this work has been asserted by him in accordance with
the Copyright, Designs and Patents Act 1988.

This book is sold subject to the condition that it shall not, by way of
trade or otherwise, be lent, resold, hired out, or otherwise circulated
without the publisher's prior consent in any form of binding or cover
other than that in which it is published and without a similar condition
including this condition being imposed on the subsequent purchaser.

CONTENTS

FOREWORD

G ravity isn't something we can see, but we can certainly feel its effects. This esoteric force has prevented humans from soaring to the highest heights since the beginning of time – the default position is that most humans will never get their feet more than a few feet off the ground, no matter how much they try.

There must be a similar force at work in the entrepreneurial world. Most businesses cannot provide a basic income to their owner, let alone create growth, profit or a valuable exit.

Statistically, self-employed people work harder, take fewer holidays, endure more stress and earn less than they would in a job. In the UK only 5% of businesses have 10 or more employees and the top 0.1% of all businesses creates 50% of the total revenue generated by all businesses! The default position is that most businesses will never get off the ground no matter how hard they try.

Defying gravity took a whole lot of smarts. Isaac Newton got the theory right in the late 1600s but it wasn't until the early 1900s that humans first took flight. Once we'd mastered the basics, we really took off. Less than 70 years after the Wright Brothers' performed a 4-mile flight we were sending men to the moon, and now about 700,000 people are airborne right this minute. With knowledge, experience, investment and design we can defy gravity and fly.

In the world of entrepreneurship, we are learning to fly, we are discovering the principles that create lift off for a business. We're discovering ways to defy the forces of entrepreneurial gravity that prevent most ideas from becoming commercially successful.

By virtue of you reading this book, I commend you for looking at the mechanics of how a business works, reading the principles of how profit is created in an entrepreneurial venture and hopefully applying the design features that create lift off.

In this book, you'll see that successful business requires you to become a key person of influence in your niche, create positive experiences, deliver exceptional value and build assets that make your venture strong. It seems like a lot of work, and it is, but it's worth it.

James Sinclair has successfully built a £10 million + business in the childcare and family entertainment industries. He writes from personal experiences, having begun as a high school dropout and built his way up to being a millionaire before the age of 30. When you meet James personally, you immediately sense his enthusiasm for life and deep curiosity for business; this book is written from that same high energy approach, making it a fun, fast-paced read. If you read this book you'll be entertained, but if you apply the ideas in this book you'll save yourself years and become more successful sooner.

When your business does take off, the view is amazing. It is possible to become a successful entrepreneur earning a top income, building a valuable asset and having a lot of fun. It's also possible to make a huge impact through business.

Many of the most successful and lucrative businesses begin with a purpose beyond making money – to make a positive impact in the world. My challenge to you is to read this book while keeping in mind the positive impact you can make for the world, not just for your shareholders.

When you get to the end of this book, be sure to act on what you discover. Be brave – some of the information requires you to step out of your comfort zone and do things differently. Have fun – building a business is a challenge of your own making and the best ideas come out when you're enjoying the process. Make a dent in the universe – we live in extraordinary times; don't waste the opportunity to do something big and meaningful.

Daniel Priestley, Co-founder of Dent
Global and Best-selling Author

INTRODUCTION

From the age of fifteen, I have had customers – real living customers. Before that, they were pretend customers in my head.

Yes, folks, I am an unusual human being. Do I care? Not in the slightest.

Being unusual gets you noticed. I am a big fan of being unusual in a usual world, and so, too, are my loyal customers.

I have always wanted to be in business. It makes up who I am. My childhood fantasies helped me build my ethos and customer service standards. At the age of eleven, I dreamt about how I would care for my customers. At twelve, I knew how my company vans would look. I remember drawing countless sketches of my logos and designs at school, dreaming about what my staff's uniform would be like – even how we would answer the phone.

I would dream without any care as to how I would finance my amazing businesses, or even build them. I just knew I wanted to build them, come what may.

Walt Disney was famous for saying, 'If you can dream it, you can build it.' This is true, but he forgot to mention *how* to do it. As the years galloped on, I gained an understanding of how money works; how companies grow; the difficulty and hard work they create; the team you need; blah, blah, blah.

I've examined the endeavours of super-successful entrepreneurs such as Walt himself – believe me, I am in awe of this bloke's achievements. I have also studied Steve Jobs, Richard Branson and a whole host of A-list business-owner entrepreneurs who have cracked the impossible nut. Taking this theory and my own experience, I've woven a customer service book into a 'How To' guide that lays down the theory for building a legacy business on any scale.

I was infected early on with the disease I call 'entrepreneurialism'. Success building isn't for everyone. It comes as a result of hard and smart work.

Let's go back to my youth. In those early days of discovery, I needed a business to occupy my mind and fulfil my destiny. I needed to make a start. I needed experience.

Trouble was, I had a passion for entertaining people. I loved magic and performance, but I also loved business. So I created an entertainment business called Partyman – a business that could turn my teenage visions into reality.

I started out as a children's entertainer, performing to families in and around London. Luckily for me, I had learned the importance of customer service through my childhood. I learned even more quickly that if I delivered experiences, I didn't have to compete on price – this was a crucial key to my early success.

As with most success-driven stories, I needed to deploy my hard-earned money into making more capital. So, I delved into other business opportunities – retail, hiring equipment, leisure, property, childcare the list goes on.

It's fair to say I fell into a trap that I believe ensnares many entrepreneurs. We start with a great plan to compete either on experience or on price, and then flit between the two. This is dangerous territory if we want long-term success. Businesses must choose – experience or price.

In my early days, people raved about the experiences I delivered as a children's entertainer and referrals came in by the truck load. The fascinating thing was that people would ring up to book a children's party, and often not ask how much I charged... they just wanted the experience. Because the experience I delivered was unique and in high demand, I could keep putting my prices up. This meant I could repeat a tried and tested model, and as a result make more money for the business. And because I never had to compromise on cost, I could deliver more value than competitors.

If you provide generalist products, you have to compete on price, and you will find yourself in an arena with key players who will have deeper pockets and bigger budgets. At the opposite end of the scale, you'll have businesses gasping for air, trying to survive, doing anything to steal custom.

Many businesses make losses on sales. After all, your customers don't really want you to make a profit – they only way they can justify the cost of something is through experience and added value. They want results. If the budget or the infrastructure is not there to create a massive company that makes profit on scale, then you'll earn wages at best.

I'll share throughout this book why I feel it's far easier and more fulfilling to create a niche business with margin, allowing you to give outstanding customer experiences. We'll learn why customers are far more loyal to experience-led businesses than price-led businesses.

Say, for example, customers are buying electrical products. Price dictates a buyer's decision, on the whole. They look for the best price, not value for money or experience. A price-led business has a customer base that will swap suppliers at the drop of a hat if a more tempting offer comes along.

The more that a business charges, the more customers expect it to do an exceptional job. If it is consistently the most expensive, then usually it is the market leader in what it does, and that builds loyalty among its customers (take Rolex, Disney and Apple, for example).

As my entrepreneurial life blossomed, so did the size of my business. So why did I forget my founding principles? Pushing aside my golden rule to compete on experience, I dived into some generalist businesses and found myself competing on price.

I'll share with you the reasons for my folly and advise you not be tempted to cross this bridge.

If entrepreneurs think they can dive into any business because they've had a run of success, they are being short-sighted. It's what I call a 'God Complex' – the idea that because you're a god of one thing, your powers can turn anything to gold. Time and time again, I have met millionaires who have one super-successful cash cow business, which they then use to fund a string of investments that they don't understand. The smart thing to do is to grow what you already have.

I have made some big boo-boos in business, and from my many lessons learned, I believe the top tip for building a successful business is to find one that has margin in the product or service you sell. Understanding margin is important. We can't put investment back into the business until we understand how much margin we need to deliver a profit. Then we can make an honest assessment as to whether to scale. And we need to face facts – some businesses cannot scale. Some will always be just about price.

To stop dallying about, you need to go into a business that you really know – something you can become the expert on. In effect, become famous for it; be twice as good as anyone else. If you genuinely love the business you have chosen, this will ooze through into whatever you create, and you'll naturally want to nurture and grow it.

Then, and only then, can you put the cherry on top by creating an experience-led business to sit in the top 20% of your market.

I like to create a scale business in an experience market which I dominate locally. When I have become the master business for a local population, then expanding, or even going global, is easier to do. I just replicate my winning formula.

This has worked for so many worldwide brands: Rolex, Rolls Royce, high-end supermarkets, etc. These guys have sailed through recessions because their customer base buys into the experience they provide, not the price.

The Vision

Now let's be realistic here – delivering great customer service costs time, money and a whole ton of devotion. It means a lot of hard work for you and your business, and you'll need a team that buys into the philosophy of your vision. Lack this, and you'll lack the grit to complete the journey. You need these tools to become the next brand leaders of the world – the next John Lewis, Disney or Rolls Royce. If that's your vision, then let's do it!

All you have to do is follow the simple rule that I know works: make a choice. Compete on experience *or* compete on price.

If you choose experience and strive to do it well, people will love you. And I don't just mean customers, I mean the lot – your team, your bankers, investors and peers, and even your competition. Customers won't look elsewhere; if you get it right, they'll become loyal fans, believe me. Then every customer becomes a marketer of your business – they will deliver more customers to your door through their referrals.

I am not talking about giving good customer service, I am talking about giving memorable customer service – stuff that people want to talk about; stuff that creates a feeling of love. If you do experiences well, you'll create a new standard, and in effect a new sector that's yours. And it'll be far less crowded than the sectors competing on price. Your enterprise will become recession-proof. You'll sail through downturns and attract the *crème de la crème* of talent to work for you, who in turn will make you and your organisation great.

It's a win-win.

So how do you survive the early battles of a growing business? If you're going to war, it's so much better to have a reason to get the troops to fight. This will be the first breakthrough I'll share in this book – telling people what you believe. If they don't believe in it too, it'll be so much easier for them to leave.

My heart breaks when start-ups, using their own capital and precious time, flop and go belly up. The most frustrating thing is it's so simple to see why they go wrong.

In the main part, the problem lies at the start – the idea. No thought has been given to a kick-ass plan to achieve profit. Furthermore, the business owner has spent less time developing his- or herself and more time just doing. It's a fact: the more we learn, the more we earn.

Too many companies are in the business of competing on price; and compete on price businesses like supermarkets make super-low margins and need massive capital reserves to become established and hit the scale required for profit.

History shows many more businesses have competed on price than experience, but take a look around and you'll notice that many more service led business have stood the test of time than their compete on price competitors.

That's because the customers of a compete on price business only have loyalty to price, so will desert a business as soon as a cheaper competitor pops up.

I've been involved in many compete on price businesses and it's nowhere near as creative or as fun as a business that competes on experience, nor does it make amazing profits without massive scale.

I have devised a set of rules for my business set up, operational and buying philosophy and I strongly advise that you do the same, this will keep you focussed as you acquire assets on your entrepreneurial journey – I'll share mine with you in the next chapter as a starting point.

In these businesses, service can get compromised because the business owner(s) wants to survive, so they cut back on all the nice stuff, like training, that creates experiences to maintain cash flow.

Price for profit so you can create experiences. It's these great customer experiences that make loyal lifelong fans for your business.

I have a revolutionary idea about business – what if we put the dream down on paper and share it every day with the 'troops', and speak about profit creation being a key ingredient to achieving it? Magic can happen when you share results with your team. Where there's profit, there's room to deliver outstanding service, and when the profits rise, the value of delivery has to rise too. The personality of the business is to deliver greatness, and this must run through it as a culture.

The Experience Business does not rip people off. We are in the business of delivering massive added value.

Creating the culture to become an Experience Business comes from the top. In my business, it comes from me, my MDS, partners and senior team. We have an obsession for delivering results to the customers that they will *love*, and someone giving my team or my brand a massive thumbs-up or five-star review means more to me than profit.

The profits will come if you care. If you take note of this book and act on its advice, you and your business will be excellent. You'll be the most expensive, because you'll be the best.

I know the potholes on the way to success, the crossroads

and the wrong turns. Together we can avoid these. This book can be your guide.

To summarise, I strongly advise that you devise a set of rules for your business set-up, operation and buying philosophy. This will keep you focused as you acquire assets on your entrepreneurial journey. As I'm a jolly nice bloke, and to say *thank you* for buying my book, I'll share my rules with you in Chapter One.

CHAPTER 1

Building a Business That Competes on Experience

During my years in business, I have caught some colds and had some decent wins. Analysis of my failures has helped me become razor sharp on making future decisions, and as a result, other people have asked me what I look for in a business.

I have a set of criteria that I now follow.

There's a well-known fact of life: we emulate what works. We copy our parents and those we surround ourselves with. Smart people choose to emulate the right people, and they move social circles if need be.

I have always tried to do the same in business: copy who's successful and emulate their success. My rules have come about as a combination of this emulation and my own frustrations at the setbacks I have experienced in the world of the entrepreneur. I feel this chapter is significant in business success – why climb a hill of treacle without a map?

'Business opportunities are like buses, there's always another one coming.'

Richard Branson

Choose the bus you wish to board carefully and harness the power to say no. You could be one bus away from your dream destination.

Common sense must prevail in business, but when we're excited about a new opportunity, it sometimes gets left at home. Business needs a clear set of criteria, *not* an impulse buy. These rules should considerably improve your chances of success in business. They are especially relevant to creating a profitable business that is easy to run – it can work with or without you – or sell, if you choose to do so. If you build your business with a view to selling it, even when that's not what you want to do, it makes for excellent discipline.

The rules allow me to deliver what I want – great customer experiences. To deliver great customer experiences, I need to be consistent, so I need a great team to make sure that happens. To build a great team, I need decent profits. And to ensure those profits long-term, I need a business that knows what it's doing and where it's going.

Let's look at the rules. I ask myself:

- Can I scale the business?

- Is the business capital intensive?

- Is there the chance for high price-tag profitable sales?

- Is there a chance for residual income?

- Is it a 'me too' business or one with high barrier to entry?

- Is there a margin in the business?

- Will people want to buy it?

- How much capital will I need to scale the business up?

- Is there a need for the business?

- After the initial set up, will it be easy to find management?

Some of the requirements you won't always hit, but you need to have a majority. In fact, the more you have, the easier you'll find it to build a successful and sustainable business.

If we can't get the grounding for the business right, we as owners won't have the time freedom to look at how our customers feel. It's all about stepping back from cash flow and profitability so we can do all the nice stuff that our team and customers will love. In effect, we want to spend more time being an entrepreneur than a doer of business.

If you become an Experience Business, you'll tick many of the rules.

Experience Businesses have high margins, they come with a

high price tag, and usually there is a way of building in residual income, even if it's creating a membership programme or billing monthly in advance. If you deliver high experiences, you can dominate a sector rather than competing with 'me too' businesses. Others will find it hard to copy you and the passion and systems you've created to keep your experience consistent.

Before we move on to how we deliver actual customer experiences, let's drill down into the nitty gritty of these rules.

Can I scale the business? Could the business, if finance wasn't an issue, easily turn over more than £2 million? Is there a demand for the product/service it provides? If your head says no, then quite simply, it's not scalable.

You may have a lovely lifestyle business that you give time and it gives you an income. Lifestyle businesses can be profitable with great margins, and it's easy for them to deliver experiences as they are largely run by a passionate owner-manager-worker. But the poor business owner will spend most of their life running the business rather than with their family; it's a time for money business.

If you want more, you need a business that you can scale. I focus this book on creating such enterprises. Choose businesses that are easy to finance.

Is the business capital intensive? Some businesses I have set up have been so capital intensive, I needed outside investment or a constant flow of cash to grow them. This is called a 'capital intensive' business, for example an airline, a chain of health clubs, hotels, etc.

This is not a deal breaker for me, but knowing what I know now, I would rather choose a scale business. If your dream is to have a capital intensive business, then you'll need to know how to raise finance to grow it. You'll need to know how to get investment, be it through sponsors, venture capitalists, crowd funding, or traditional routes such as bank loans.

One pro of capital intensive businesses is that they are not 'me too' – people don't automatically think, *Yes, I could do that*. Only the bigger players can copy a capital intensive business, and by copying it, they will also consider buying it. And this is the second pro – you have a real asset that's easier to market for sale.

However, I hate the pressure a capital intensive business puts on you to grow, even if you're doing really well. Traditional lenders like you to pay one loan off before you start again, or you will be tempted to give up equity in return for cash to grow – something I hate. Where possible, it's better to own and borrow until you are really ready to take equity investment.

Examples of scale businesses that do not need capital to grow are insurance brokers and recruitment companies, but they could also be considered 'me too' businesses.

Is there the chance for high price-tag profitable sales? You may not have the capacity to implement all the rules, but if you can get both high and low price-tag sales, you'll win. That way, you can serve the people who love you so well that they will invest in the products or services that you really make a profit from.

Look at Apple. These guys have iTunes – low price residual sales and subscriptions to keep regular cash coming in, but their computers and iPads are high price profitable sales.

Another killer example is to look at theme parks. If people really love the rides, they will buy a ticket at three times the face value simply to queue jump. On top of that, the park can sell hotel space and five star experiences.

My last and favourite example is from the Entrepreneurs' Network. One of our members is a trusted local estate agent, and we discussed building one-off profitable sales by selling houses, then developing the letting agency arm to earn tons of residual income. The aim is to get enough residual income to pay the bills so that all house sales are pure profit.

Is there a chance for residual income? My favourite of all favourites is the chance to build a business that has residual or recurring income. It's the fandabidozi goal of business – crack this and so many things will click into place. You'll have less stress, do less marketing, make less effort to find new customers. Your business will be highly attractive to sell, and it'll be super easy to raise finance again.

Landlords invest in property because they know they will receive recurring monthly income once they've found their tenant (customer). This needs to be applied to business if possible.

Once you have marketed to the prospects, they become customers. Then as long as you do a great job, they stay with you and become raving fans who pay you every month. Then you know what money's coming in. My favourite recent business is Netflix. Literally millions of customers pay it a monthly fee of £6.

Build a business with residual income and you'll discover the stress buster of business.

Is it a 'me too' business or one with high barrier to entry?
One of my Entrepreneurs Network members is a dentist who does a specific type of cosmetic dentistry. Becoming a cosmetic dentist is no easy task, if I decided tomorrow that I wanted to eat his lunch by setting myself up as a dentist then I couldn't. I'd need to go and spend a few years at Dentist school before I can get started.

It's the same in some of my businesses. I started in play centres, but found it was too easy for competitors to open up in the same town.

Think hotels. 'I want to build a B and B.'

'Me too! I can do that.'

Versus: 'I want to build a hotel with 300 rooms, pool, gym and sauna.'

'OK, not me too.'

If your business is easily copied then there's much more chance you're going to start seeing some pressure on your prices, competing with new entrants and fighting for minimal profits.

Once I went into childcare and outdoor attractions I made it much harder for competitors to move into my market. Marsh Farm is 70 acres, nobody's going to build a similar attraction near me and start nibbling away at my lunch.

Whatever I'm thinking of doing, I ask "is it a 'me too' business or one with high barrier to entry?"

Is your business so easily copied that you will end up competing on price and fighting for minimal profits? Choose something that is so big that people can't copy you easily. Seriously, the bigger you think, the less crowded the market space will be.

Is there a low labour cost to turnover ratio? We turn now to how some businesses have higher labour costs to turnover ratios that others.

Many start-ups chose their particular trade because it's something they love to do, or they have experience in that sector. Far better to choose from the outset with an investor's approach rather than an entrepreneur's approach. Yes, choose something you love, but choose something that's not massively labour intensive, especially at conception.

Businesses don't go bust because of lack of passion and will; they go bust because the person as the top hasn't educated and worked on him- or herself as well as they could, or because the overheads get the better of them. In other words, they run out of cash.

Believe me, choosing something that has the lowest labour to turnover ratio will certainly stand you in good stead to grow the business. In times of peril – and there will always be times of peril in any business – not having to worry about a big labour bill is a sure winner. I have businesses that have labour to turnover ratios of 50% and others that only have 10%.

A really important KPI for systemising a business is to work out a good level of labour your business can afford compared to its turnover (you will find via a simple internet search the industry standard for your sector), implement it into your structure and keep to it. Measure it every day, week and month. If you're going over your fixed percentage point, you will know problems are hitting your business.

You never want to understaff, but this happens all too often. A chance to increase profits one month by controlling costs could be to the detriment of your future in customer experience – remember, we are building a customer experience business that's consistent.

Do you need lots of expensive staff to grow the business?

Paying people what they're worth is a whole lot easier if you're established and making plenty of profit, but building a business usually burns tons of cash and everything makes a loss in the early days. It's a business owner's job to break even as quickly as possible and then speed the process to profit.

This is the same with staff. Team members all lose us money when they start – they take training; they need investing in. Speeding them up to break even all needs to be in the businesses operation plan. A good measure is ninety days to get a team member fired up to knowing your business.

Think of a scalable business with easy-to-train team members rather than those who demand big salaries. Recruit people with attitude and train them the way you want. In time, as profit grows, reward these people with higher salaries and perks so they become your tomorrow leaders.

Coffee shops, for example, start staff as baristas, then make them shop managers, then area managers. In effect, they create a culture of progression that is home grown.

I spent a whole day with Pret A Manger and met the training director. When I arrived, I noticed the training offices looked fun and interactive – like being in a Pret shop. There, Pret teaches its staff how to make coffee and serve sandwiches in a way that reflects the vision the company has. Above the entrance are the words: 'The next CEO of Pret A Manger could walk through these doors'.

I was blown away by this ethos. Even the lowest paid staff could run the company one day.

Pret is now an international £billion business which has all the expensive staff it needs. But when it started, it was a sandwich shop run by two guys with a big vision that was never compromised. As a result, both staff and customers rewarded them by building the business to what it is now.

Controlling overheads is a key skill in business, and we must remember that our biggest overhead walks on two legs. So does our biggest investment. It's essential we build our team to be amazing and lean to stay in the game.

I'll delve deep into team building later.

Is there a margin in the business? If your business does not have margin, then it's going to be mighty difficult to scale it and make decent profits. This is where the price-led businesses sit.

Price-led businesses need a huge turnover to make a million clear profit, so they're looking for every bugger to buy from them. There are plenty of businesses that have profit margins of just 1–3%, which is not for me. I look for margins of at least 20%, and preferably 50%.

Pricing for profit is essential. Never price for sales if you want to build an Experience Business

Will people want to buy it? Build a business to sell, even if you don't want to sell it. Asking yourself every day whether someone would buy your business is a great habit. With that in mind, you're sure to make profits. Your systems and disciplines will stay high.

But here's the thing: some business sectors are much more sellable than others. Funnily enough, the ones that follow my rules tend to be the ones that the market wants to buy.

For example, I have been involved heavily in leisure chain businesses, which are much harder to sell compared to, say, a chain of day nurseries or a successful insurance company. The latter two businesses have a huge market appeal. Start-up entrepreneurs often forget this, or simply don't know it, whereas seasoned investors always invest in a business that will sell easily if it's profitable.

If you have the luxury of starting from scratch, I would highly recommend you do some research into finding what business niches are sellable. I did not start my first business with this rule in mind, so I needed to implement it retrospectively. It was what made me add a childcare business on to all my leisure sites, so if I wanted to sell, then I'd attract a lot more buyers.

Always build a business to sell, even if you don't want to sell it. It's an essential discipline of successful entrepreneurs.

How much capital will I need to scale the business? Believe me, as a business grows it can burn cash like nothing else. Poof! Profits gone.

It's actually the reason people go bust. Why? Because they want their business to be great so put operations before sales. Then they see the growth is not profitable and downscale the business back to where everything was lovely. In rough terms, all businesses have levels at which the next infrastructure/ operation needs to go in place, and this sucks profit until the sales catch up. And trouble comes if you don't have the cash to finance these stages.

Now if you are averse to taking loans or finance or selling a chunk of equity and you choose to grow the business out of cash flow, you'll sail close to the wind.

Growth – aggressive growth rather than organic growth – must be financed by investment and outside cash rather than turnover. So the best thing to do is to choose a business that needs low capital to grow. We can then grow the business as an experience-led one that customers will love so they'll pay 30–100% more than they would to the weak price-led businesses in our niche.

For example, say you want to build either a nightclub chain or a personal training company.

For the personal training company, the objective is to find the best people, notified experts in the field, to deliver the best experience, then build it to be a £2 million company that makes £500,000 profit. This is achievable. The investment will be low, say £100k start-up costs, but hard work and marketing are essential. To grow and scale the business, you will need to bring in more customers and teams via turnover investment, but this will be low and can be turned on and off as cash allows.

Let's say your nightclub will turn over the same money and make the same profits, but the capital investment to start it is £1.5 million, and you will need the same amount every five years. Plus, to scale the business to multiple locations, you will need the same start-up costs again. As soon as you have a second nightclub, you need another area management team.

Growth must be funded, and that's great as long as you can accept outside investment. If you think having partners is tough, choose an industry you can grow without a regular massive injection of cash. Even if you do have an abundance of cash, trust me – it's far better to choose a business niche that does not need mass capital investment to grow.

The richest man I know scaled a massive business in insurance. He didn't need capital to grow the business; hard work and outstanding customer service built his £60million company. The same concept applies to recruitment, a business I am involved in. It's easy to scale with low capital.

However, capital intensive businesses are less 'me too' than a recruitment company, for example, so if you're averse to outside investment, try to choose something that needs a manageable amount of initial capital, but not masses more to scale after the start-up phase.

In my experience, raising the first capital is easy. Banks will lend it, or you may have savings or take equity out of property. It gets difficult when you need to raise the same amount again to finance the growth. Banks call this over trading. They would rather you pay back what you owe and start again with a new facility. Entrepreneurs who are serious movers and shakers don't like to do this, so choose a business that is not so capital intensive.

Is there a need for the business? Some businesses will be easier to finance than others. Banks, investors and venture capitalists have an appetite to lend to one business rather than another, even if they both make a profit and their future looks rosy.

For example, it will be easy to grow a vehicle hire company as banks *love* tangible assets that can be sold. Plus, there is always a need for the product and/or service. If a company makes a unique product, it could be viewed by investors as here today and gone tomorrow, even if it's currently making lots of profit. The risk is if the company goes south, who will buy its assets or business?

Choosing a sector that is easy to finance gets a big tick from me.

After the initial set up, will it be easy to find management?
Some businesses are too key man. I learned this from my entertaining days: I couldn't sack and replace myself because I *was* the business. People wanted me.

Through my business mentoring company, the Entrepreneurs' Network, I am blessed to spend time with aspiring, super-successful and, indeed, frustrated entrepreneurs. One of my recent phone calls was with a smart man who had built a highly profitable dentist chain in a short space of time. He was making an ultra-high profit on his turnover, but he was still a dentist. His frustration was that he wanted to be a business owner.

He was on track because he had made the mental shift to do this, but crucially he couldn't find a replacement for himself in his business. He was so specialist that only a handful of people in the UK could do what he did.

We discussed a strategy to overcome this, settling on creating an in-house training programme for aspiring dentists to take the reins in a couple of years so he could first become a CEO, then an owner with a CEO in place.

To summarise, you want to be in the business full-time to get it going, but be ready to sack yourself as soon as you can. If that's not possible, then it's not the right business.

Wahoo! We now know the rules I use to assess any business I'm looking to set up or take over. If you're already in business, trust me here – if possible, implement some of these rules. They will deliver remarkable improvements.

Now let's look into how my team and I create Experience Businesses.

CHAPTER 2

Vision, Mission and Culture

A powerful vision that will stand the test of time is what makes great people work for great companies. Then customers align their beliefs with that company and buy from it. A super mission statement breaks the vision down into manageable objectives to achieve each part of it. Manageable chunks, people.

But the key is to share the company's vision. This is powerful because people who work for you can then choose whether to believe in the company. Some may not be aligned to the vision. Maybe it's too much. In this case, if you can't change the people's minds, you must change the people.

This is closely followed by creating a culture for your company that's aligned to the vision and mission. I primarily wrote this book as a guide for new team members so they could understand how my family of companies delivers the outstanding customer experience we continually work to achieve, and to remind people who lose their way about our vision, mission and culture.

I like to think of vision, mission and culture like this: a vision is a fifty-year plan, a mission is a ten year plan and a culture is a daily plan.

You now know that Customer Experience Businesses are my preference over generalist price-led businesses. Experience Businesses excited me when I started out at the age of fifteen, and they still excite me. As a result, my vision for all my companies is this:

> To be the world leaders in customer experience by creating brands that our customers love. We are proud of what we do. People become so excited by us that they not only choose us, they are our loyal fans.

I read this vision statement again and again; it's the bedrock of all my companies and the Entrepreneurs' Network. Anything I put time or money into must have this powerful vision.

I'm passionate about customer service, and as a youngster was so in awe of companies which delivered experiences that created memories, that ethos became part of my being. I wanted to be in that space, and this gave me a distinct advantage – it's part of my why. It's my company vision.

Now as a leader-entrepreneur of hundreds of team members, my job is to get this message across to them. I want every team member in every department to be memory makers – I want them to be creators of great customer experiences, so much so I renamed Customer Service 'Customer Experience'. Heck, I even put it in people's job titles, like 'catering customer experience manager'. My obsession with making my customers happy filters down to my team. We are passionate as an organisation about our brand promise to deliver outstanding customer experience.

Your team may coin a certain phrase, such as the 'Disney way' or the 'Virgin way'. One of my greatest achievements is when a team member says 'that's the 'Partyman way' or 'that's the Entrepreneurs Network way'. I can't begin to tell you how much of a firework moment that is. If people within your organisation start saying that they don't do things other people's way, they do it 'your way', you have an amazing organisation and great people working for you.

If you have decided to deliver great experiences through your business and you have a burning desire to achieve this, you jolly well will. If you truly believe in your vision, you have far more chance of it spreading as a culture in your team. And the great thing is it's not hard to do. It doesn't require massive expenditure; it's a culture, pure and simple, and it's up to you as a leader to breed that culture at all levels and practise it every day.

However, this is where it often goes wrong. In so many growing businesses, customer service is forgotten, but it's the companies that practise this crucial part of the business which have sustainability and a giant tribe of loyal fans both internally (team) and externally (customers).

It's the simple stuff that creates experiences, and it's the simple stuff that people love. It's being memory makers; being unusual; being human a world that's becoming less personnel and more automated. In effect, treat your customers like your grandma and you'll win.

At Partyman, we say 'The difference between ordinary and extraordinary is just a little extra.' It's all about creating a relationship between customer and team member, nothing more. Now we just have to know how to build that relationship.

Lots of businesses offer good service, but it doesn't get remembered or generate waves of testimonials. Bad service gets remembered and great service gets remembered as both have the same powerful force behind them – they create a reaction. You choose which one you want for your company.

If you're one of the majority of business owners delivering good customer service most of the time, with a little bit more effort, your systems and processes could become great. Just 10% above good will get you noticed and recognised as providing a great experience. The real hard work is keeping the great experience consistent, especially when the original owner is no longer running the day to day operations of the business. This is why training and development needs to happen every day. It is essential to make sure the experience stays at a level where people are happy to pay a higher price for it. Dip below that level and you're back to competing on price. Even worse, if your fans bring their friends into your flock, they will get seriously pissed off if you dip below the standards that made them fall in love with your customer experience.

Despite what people think, customers are prepared to pay more for things that deliver experience. Fact.

My work life kicked off as an entertainer. It helped that I loved performing – creating the ultimate birthday party experience was a like taking a duck to water for me. I wanted to be the best, but not necessarily the busiest or the most expensive. I did become the busiest and the most expensive in my area, though, and I did this because I delivered a unique experience which could not be generalised or copied by competition.

Since then, I have gone on to grow my companies to employ 350 people, turn over £millions and look after over a million guests each year. It's through running these businesses that my ethos has spread through the very fabric of my companies.

Before we delve into the tips and tricks to place experiences at the heart of your team's ethos, let's look at the levels of service and make a decision of where your business currently sits.

Customer experience levels

In my opinion there are four levels of customer service: crap, average, generalist/good and customer experience.

The lower you are on the ladder, the more you will compete

on price. Low prices might attract more customers, but why not sell to loyal fans instead? Why not make your business into a celebrity whom everyone wants to hang out with?

Crap customer service. This business competes with tons of others and lowers its price to get its sales. Customers hate buying from it and will only do so as a last resort. A business cannot survive in this way

Average customer service. Many established businesses end up delivering average service. Customers are not aware of anything outstanding; they just rock up and buy. The business competes on price and will have a low percentage of profit in relation to turnover.

Competition comes and goes when you're on this step of the ladder. Team members do not think the company is visionary, and nor does the management, leader, whoever. The teams work to collect a pay packet, and the extent of their training would have been shadowing an existing team member on their first day with the company.

Good/generalist customer service. Some of you may have the fortune to be in a generalist business with a massive brand and plenty of cash. If this is the case it will be difficult for you to invest in consistent experience as you will lack the margin to create it. So it's better to deliver a consistently good service to compete with other generalist businesses that do not do it so well. I am a big fan of consistency.

People would rather use you than an average business, but will still shop on price. The team will be aware that good customer service is a belief of the company, and the management will pull them up on sub-standard service. Training will be delivered annually, and perhaps even quarterly.

Customer experience. This is the holy grail of business delivery, not only because it's more profitable, but because it feels great to be in this area. I am even enjoying writing this point far more than the other three.

People can easily become customers, but what you want are loyal fans who fall in love with your company and buy from you because of past experience. They trust you, and know that even if you muck up, you will go to the ends of the earth to put it right.

But for this to happen, your business – the team, leader, owner – needs to love its customers. Then they become guests, or even family. . At the time of buying, they feel like they are your most important customer, and they can't wait to tell the world that they bought from you.

This is the glory of an Experience Business – the customer becomes a fan who markets for you, sticks up for you and raves about you.

Educate + Congratulate + Appreciate × Repeat = Experience

I believe in this as a steadfast rule.

Team members will fully understand the leader's vision and make it their own. The managers are on point; they see their culture as making the leadership vision come true. Training is given on average for fifteen minutes a day. The business loves training its people, and the people who work for it love the training. It is a systemised machine and everyone knows exactly their required output.

The business leaders believe in Educate + Congratulate + Appreciate × Repeat = Experience.

The educating of your team on the values, culture, mission and vision of your company is the key to successful experience delivery. Often in un-regulated businesses where training isn't mandatory, it's not regarded as a priority. An experience-led company believes the better the training, the better the staff become, and that leads to a better experience for the owners, team members and customers. Experience-led companies constantly scrutinise their training and look to improve.

Humanity

When building a system, we must make sure everything is as human as possible. This sounds contradictory – building a system generally involves a machine, but it's similar to the reason why companies need both leadership and management. Leaders (entrepreneurs) dream things up; managers systemise everything to be consistent. Especially when we're running a business of scale, the dreams will never come true without a systemised approach. But without a human approach, dreams are soon forgotten. Entrepreneurs want their dreams to be ongoing and consistent.

Consistency becomes the foundation for excellence in both an experience-led and price-led business, and excellence in an experience-led organisation is found in a consistently human approach. So the compromise between systemisation and humanisation is consistency of delivery.

A large part of what you will achieve will be done by being consistently as human as possible and systemising this as a culture in the business. The old-fashioned human touch makes for great business sense if you're wanting to be remembered as it is now seen as unusual. Hardly any businesses put human interaction as a priority; they want to automate everything. Automation is great, but not at the expense of customer service experience.

Wherever possible, make your customers feel special, allow them choice, veer off the guidelines, even just a little. This really gets you noticed and has extreme power. It's easy for a small business to do, but more challenging for a bigger business. But it's not impossible; it just needs an agreed system.

For example, if you owned a small coffee and sandwich shop and you wanted to love your customers, you could spontaneously give them their order for free every now and then. Imagine the value this would create; imagine the lifetime customer memory. Giving without receiving creates a bond. Good small businesses have always done this.

Big businesses do this as well, but it's too system led. It's likely to be 'Stamp the card ten times and your next one will be free' or 'Collect points and get this when you have so many'. What if a big business acted like a small business? That would make waves.

Pret A Manger, the international sandwich maker and quality fast food chain, is a global £billion+ business. It is systematised to the max, but without a doubt it has made sure that customers become fans. How? Because its product servers are encouraged to be human. They can give free food and drinks to regular customers or people that they like, or indeed someone who's had a bad day. Imagine going into a giant international business and the person serving you says, 'You look lovely today, have this one on us.' Wow.

Customer service cuddles

How can we create such love for our brand that our customers say thank you? Disney actually gets customers to queue up for hours just for cuddles from team members dressed as their favourite characters. And the best part is they take a photo, make it their profile picture on social media, place it on the mantelpiece and show their friends. Disney will spend millions on a ride, but will this be talked about as much as the day customers met the mouse in the red trousers? It's the human interaction that gets remembered. That's the part which will turn your customers into fans.

My belief is that when anyone does business with my companies, they will love the facilities, love the offer, but above all, they will love the team. In effect, they love the culture. If you manage to employ great people who totally buy into the company vision, you will retain fans. You will see repeat business fly through the door, and you won't need to market as much as your customers will do it for you by sharing your memory making experiences.

I cannot emphasise enough how much your people make your brand. My favourite old restaurant, Alvaros, is a little Portuguese gem. The place looks like my Nan's front room with old furniture and old wallpaper, but you wouldn't believe the business it does. It is totally overbooked; getting a table on a Saturday is a near miracle. The restaurant even closes for two weeks a year so the owners can go on holiday together as a family. In a seven-day-week world, how many businesses dare to dictate their own opening times?

The answer is special businesses that compete on experience. These businesses have the most loyal of fans who feel love from the people serving them. The food in Alvaros is good, but the service is something quite sensational. Staff open doors and pull out chairs for customers, their uniforms are always clean, they tell jokes and remember people's names. And yes, there are cuddles too. This all creates loyalty.

This restaurant is an example of a business that offers consistent experience, and it also ticks my rule of creating margin to deliver the experience. It can charge double the price of a normal restaurant and people pay willingly because it's consistent. It's like a theatre, everyone playing a part in a beautiful story.

Customer service, and I mean exceptional customer service, becomes an experience. Humans are the start and end to achieving this, but aesthetics – branding, uniforms – helps too. It gives your people an image; if you like, a prop to make the show better. When you're flying first class, you appreciate the surroundings because of outstanding human attention to detail. The luxuries are the props that set the scene for the show; the staff are the all-important actors.

It takes two

Building an experience business requires two people. In fact, that's my winning formula. An entrepreneur – a proper one, that is – will pay little attention to detail. They are like GPS who know a lot about everything, but don't specialise in any one thing. For that, they pass you on to the experts. Similarly, an entrepreneur needs to diagnose each of the business's 'illnesses' then employ experts to deal with them. And these experts, ladies and gentlemen, are managers.

Very rarely do you see an entrepreneur successfully filling the role of manager. Personally, I have the big ideas, raise finance, get deals done, research and direct. In effect, I install my vision and make it happen. That is my job. The entrepreneur roles the dice, takes the risk and leads the quarter to quarter, year to year, decade to decade decisions. He or she is the objective setter.

Now it's time for the grand master in the journey to enter – the CEO; the MD; the manager. The manager is just as important as the entrepreneur. If the entrepreneur decides where to go, the manager decides how to get there.

Respect for each other's roles is paramount. The entrepreneur must support the manager's decisions and align to the consistency the manager wants to install. Entrepreneurs will flit in and out of ideas, so the manager must only allow the best to get through and complete objectives before the entrepreneur flourishes further. A great entrepreneur knows to listen to the manager's advice, and the manager must listen to the entrepreneur in return. They will know each other's weaknesses and fill in for each other, pushing each other to greater things.

This understanding between entrepreneur and manager has been essential my success. I found my right hand man and trusted friend, advisor and mentor, in my first company, sacrificing profits to pay him in the early days. That's right – he earned from the company when I did not as he made building my dream so much easier.

A talented entrepreneur surrounds him- or herself with people far more talented than him or her. Great managers are attracted to great entrepreneurs and vice versa.

Once you have got your dynamic duo, it's time to build your dream team.

CHAPTER 3

Recruiting Your Team

Recruit on attitude first, then on skillset.

If you are a small enterprise and you find someone good to work with, nurture, cuddle and hold them. Commit them to your vision. Share your ethos – how great you want to become as a company and how great you want them to become.

Think mentorship and you're on the right path.

You pay to get your employees' time, but a top leader will get more for their company. They will have their employees' hearts too. (That concept is not my own, by the way. It comes from one of the wisest businessmen I know – a man I am pleased to call a friend. Thanks, Andrew.) Achieve this and your people will consistently deliver an experience that your guests/customers/visitors will love.

The fact is you can only mentor so many people yourself. As

your company grows, the whole team will need to mentor every new team member who comes in. This brings about a culture.

Most companies employ people on a swap-time-for-money basis. Good companies get both employees' time and their loyalty – a band of employees with an ambition to stick around and climb the ranks, doing the best they can for the company. Then employees are more like partners; they are fiercely loyal and proudly tell their family and friends that they love working for the company.

Disney, in my view, are the gods of creating this working environment. They attract great people who already have the 'I want to work for Disney' attitude; they suck them in like a magnet. Imagine having potential employees who can't wait to work for you.

Like a great university or school, there's a lot to be said for broadcasting your company's strengths, even if it's just for employee attraction. Every time I read about something that such a company is doing, it reminds me of the way we do things, even though the likes of Apple and Ferrari are slightly more corporate than a clown from Essex.

So, do I have any tips for picking up great people? Let's kick off with enrolling the right people into your organisation. I say 'enrol' deliberately as the aim is to educate them to understand your company's processes before they graduate. Think like a university – or as close as you can get to it. Universities recruit on attitude as well as skillset, just like the Experience

Business does. So ask potential employees, 'Are you a happy person?' That's right, folks, you want to assess whether they're a personality fit for your company.

Employ happy, motivated, well-rounded people, and their attitude will rub off on average people, raising them up too. The more naturally positive people you have around you, the higher your chances will be of squashing the negativity that lurks in so many companies.

My problem has always been taking over existing companies that are harbouring bad eggs – people who procrastinate and drift away during their first meeting with me. The first meeting that should be full of joy and happiness. If that happens to you, you'll remember it. Then you look to manage the person, helping them either to embrace your ethos or to move on.

Whatever business you are in, get people to attend a trial day and observe them.

Do they naturally seem willing and open? Do you warm to them? Be wowed by personality rather than skillset. Trust your gut. An over-skilled person with the wrong attitude can destroy an organisation's culture

Find out what culture they like to be around. Does this fit with yours? Recruiting is a de-selection process as much as a selection one. Your recruitment journey allows both parties to decide if the relationship will work.

Make it clear from the outset that you want a long relationship.

Employees need to be on board. This is how the Experience Business ticks.

Some of my best people have been with me since I started the company, and that's because we get what each other believes. We want to achieve the same things. And I see the future of my companies in the people we bring on.

Enrol people with your beliefs. But don't employ another you. Entrepreneurs make, in my experience, awful managers. We want people who are organised, can deal with difficult decisions, have ideas, are skilled with numbers, can execute a plan. A mix of skillsets is essential.

The Experience Business does everything really well. This is why you need a combination of people. Think of an orchestra. It wouldn't work with forty-five conductors; we need the full ensemble of strings, bass and brass.

Look for your culture in others, yes, but not yourself.

Hire slowly (and fire fast). Take your time to hire. The process takes as long as it takes. A favourite phrase of mine when I'm hiring a key person is: 'We'll wait till the right person is found'.

The cost of a bad team member can be astronomical. I would far rather stay with the team I have than upset the apple cart with a bright young thing who can't last the distance.

We have a long-term approach to finding people in my companies. We plan in advance, saying, 'In twelve or twenty-four months, we will need to find X to take us to the next level.' If we find that particular talent before the crunch point, we'll take them on.

Conducting multiple interviews, at least three, makes for good grounding.

Also, I've learned through experience that it's worth interviewing a couple of people at a higher salary level than you're planning on appointing at. Say you're looking to appoint someone at £40,000 a year, I'd ask my recruiter to find me a couple of candidates who are looking for £60,000, just to let me understand what I'd get for my money at the next price point up.

Sometimes, I've found that a relatively small step up in salary level can mean finding someone with significantly more experience or expertise, easily able to justify a bigger package than I was planning on and deliver a significant return.

Panic employment happens in most companies at some point. My companies fall into this trap occasionally, and I hate that we do. As a seasonal business, we have to graft to find corkers and train them, only for them to leave at the end of the season. The rule of thumb is that it takes ninety days to get an employee singing from the same hymn sheet as the company, and if a season lasts ninety days, they leave just as they're up to speed. So I try to find a secondary income to retain my core employees out of season.

The stronger your business, the less you'll have to panic

employ. Entrepreneurs panic employ when they've grown the business to such an extent that they need a team for a wave of new turnover to be managed. Continuity of team breeds consistency, and consistency breeds customer experience. Customers then become fans and you've won, my friend.

Customer experience needs investment, particularly a good chunk of the business owner's time to get it going. It's usually the tiniest of things that make a difference to your business – opening doors for people, the way you answer the phone, name badges, smiles, presentation, music and interaction. Look for employees who naturally have these traits, and the best way to do this is to set up a Discovery Day.

The Discovery Day

This could also be called the Audition. Whether you're hiring for one special position or a number of positions, if you take the Discovery Day approach, you'll undoubtedly have a far greater chance of finding a star.

To create the Discovery Day, get the key decision makers involved. They are the judges, remembering above all else that the Experience Business's secret weapon is naturally happy people. This process helps you find the right attitude first, then you discover what the people can bring to the table.

For this process, you'll need to welcome recruits warmly. Your initial approach should give them a flavour of what the position is about – this will whittle out the 'No, this is not for me' people.

In your recruitment ads, deliver a quick bio of your company, given by you as Founder or the Directors, if possible. Talk about your history and future plans, and the opportunities you'll be able to offer the best people. Make it sound like a story. I like to give case studies of people who have climbed the ranks to positions of leadership and management.

Share a truth, too. For example: 'Even if you're not selected today, you'll still get a chance to learn a process and have some fun, and you'll discover if we are right for you.' Invite the recruits on stage to talk about themselves. Take notes, and remember the ones you are drawn to.

Next create a series of tasks for the group that are relevant to the role. I've set out some examples below.

Task 1. Role play time. Tell your recruits, 'You've just been given a ten-minute spot at a seminar to pitch our product or service to 1,000 warm buyers.'

Get them to write down the headings for their prompts and give them time to put together a powerful talk. The ones who have researched your company will be best prepared for this.

If public speaking will be essential for the role, you'll want to see how powerfully they can pitch.

Task 2. Write an article for an industry magazine on why your product or service is so good that people should buy it. The internet is ready and waiting for everyone to be publicists of their product, so good copy writing is generally a key skill.

Task 3. Sketch an advert for a magazine. Here you'll see what knowledge the recruits have of advertising and creating the compelling headings needed for customers to take action. Get them to talk through what prompted them to design their advert in this way.

Task 4. Ask the recruits to create a brainstorm diagram of how they're going to get to market – the steps they need to take, whom they need to meet and how they will forge relationships. Supply giant paper and pens for them to do this.

Each recruit then has to present their steps to the others. You'll see the people who have a natural flair for your company's ethos that you can mould and improve on. Walk around and ask questions as people do the work, and involve your existing team too.

For a Discovery Day, you'll need enough room for everyone to feel comfortable, a PA system, water, mints, and a good lunch. Most importantly, you'll need an MC to keep the buzz going. Observe even in the breakout sessions how the recruits interact. You may find more than one star.

This stuff works, so it's worth the effort.

Headhunting

My best people have come through my network. If I've got to know someone over a number of years, when we meet it's not an interview, it's a natural process.

Falling in love when I least expect it is the ultimate high in my life, and I've come pretty close to this feeling with team members I have found. Headhunting can reveal amazing people who can add impact to your company. People you'll love.

Traditionally, headhunting would be done in collaboration with a headhunting firm. Now the correct way is to do it yourself, and get your team ready to seek talent too. My team members have recommended future recruits to me, so tell your teams that if they know someone great, bring them forward.

Great people have also come from companies I've collaborated with or worked for over the years, and from competitors I have met at industry events. Sometimes their people like my approach better and want to come into my family of companies. I have also seen great people in action when I've been out, and boom! I've offered them a job.

So, does it really work? At the time of writing, the entire Entrepreneurs' Network team has come from headhunting. The result is a well-oiled machine with no weak links. The team loves the customers and the company.

With headhunting, you find what you actually need, not what

you might need. It's more of a sure thing – you've assessed the person and seen them doing well. It's far better to pay someone you know will be great and make things happen rather than waiting for ninety days to train a new recruit, especially if you're like me and some of your companies are a little quirky.

And if someone doesn't believe in what the company wants to achieve, politely ask them to leave. If the people can't change, change the people.

CHAPTER 4

Pricing + Consistency = Profit

Pricing your business for profit

Pricing is the ultimate key to longevity in business. The trick to achieving high price sales is to have predetermined buyers in your niche. This means people knowing you're the best, and to be the best, you have to deliver consistently.

But the cost of being the best is sometimes not factored in.

As a rule of thumb, you want to have the highest possible gross profit to allow you to innovate and invest time, money and energy into the niche you operate in so you continue to be a leader. Gross profit gives you a real steer on how you price things up – the bigger the margin, the more chance you have of producing strong net profits.

A lot of people think that gross profit is the net margin they will make, and they feel they will be ripping people off if they aim for a high margin, or people simply won't become customers. But they will if the product is excellent. Getting pricing for profit on point is the only way you can build an Experience Business that will stand the test of time.

I always where possible educate my team about how and why we seek high margins in the products we sell when we compete on experience.

Money doesn't grow on trees

But it can be understood. I am a massive fan of educating my team on how cash is burned in a business, but I struggled to explain the difference between a gross margin and a net profit till I implemented the tree presentation.

While sitting with my catering team, I came up with a plan. We were on a sticky wicket – they weren't following the formula I had set for pricing food. Instead, they were thinking we would be quids in if we reduced our costs. They didn't understand how the business burned so much cash – they thought I was being greedy and profiteering.

So I came up with the cash flow tree of profit, a set of workings, always accurate and closely aligned to what the monthly profit and loss looked like. With these workings, I showed what we'd spent on product, labour, heating, planning time, loan interest, depreciation and the like. It was crucially important that the workings were as accurate as possible. I wanted the tree to be as close to the truth as it could be to help my team understand the pricing formula I use. The leaves of the tree represented cash. We armed ourselves with a set of sharp cutting instruments, and we were away.

Gathering the team around the tree, I played a game.

'Welcome, team. I am going to show you that money does grow on this tree. It represents our monthly or daily income, and the scissors represent overheads that will take some of the tree. I would like you guys to guess what you think things cost.

'Let's play. How much do you think we pay in sales tax?'

They answered, say, 20%, so I lopped off 20% of the leaves.

'How much do you think we pay for labour?'

I lopped off another 35%, as the team suggested.

'How much do you think we pay in rent?'

They gave their answer, and I chopped off another 10%.

When we got down to four leaves, I said, 'You know, we haven't paid for any product to sell yet.'

The leaves lying on the floor is a dramatic demonstration of all the costs of running a business. No amount of spreadsheets, email bombardment, telephone calls, conference speeches or face to face meetings illustrate the point as well as my tree of profit does.

The point I want to get across is that a business needs a healthily high gross profit margin if they want to stay in the game. You can't build a sustainable business within investing in training, infrastructure, people and development.

Create your bibles

There are three rules of a business, regardless of its size, regardless of its pricing architecture – whether it's 'stack 'em high, sell 'em quick' or sell for a margin and deliver experience:

- An entrepreneur builds a business that allows him or her to be sacked as soon as possible

- The business should become as systemised and documented as flying a plane

- Consistency, consistency, consistency.

I can't emphasise enough that consistency is the rule of rules. When a business delights, it must do so consistently to maintain customer flow. If you offer a 'vanilla' service, then that's OK, but it must be consistently vanilla.

The worst thing to do is to compete on price then not maintain your standards because profits won't allow it. It's far smarter to be OK consistently than have moments of glory sporadically.

Consistency leads to longevity of customer retention. If you crack it, you're made. It's what the customer desires. No one wants a yo-yo service driven by a business owner who constantly changes their mind. This is why steady management plays such a key role in consistency.

So once you've started your business, it's a good idea to create a Business Operations Bible. Along with the Brand Bible, it tells your great story. You'll need both.

The Operations Bible will be the 'how to' of your company's operations: a step by step guide to the running of the business – without you in it. This is exactly what makes a scalable business consistent. The phrase 'if you want a job done well, do it yourself' needs to be banned from your organisation. If the owner/entrepreneur has to be the superhero saving the day to keep operations running consistently, then the business is not scalable.

This is why the Operations Bible must be detailed to the last point. The effort needed to build this document is vast – the best businesses, whether they compete on experience or price, document their every moment ready to scale the business without the founders.

I am again reminded of the day I met the training manager for Pret A Manger, the worldwide sandwich business. This company has an Operational Manual the size of the *Encyclopaedia Britannica*. It includes:

- How to sweep the front of the store

- Which spoon to use for serving egg mayonnaise

- How often the floor must be cleaned

- How to give free drinks away

- How to answer the phone.

It was built to be dummy proof, and the instructions are followed religiously.

My first entertainment business was me. I was the product and the only person who had any involvement in operations. If one person runs a micro business, their brain and actions are the consistent service that drives custom. The second someone else joins, an Operations Bible must be built.

Where consistency flows, the customer goes.

How to build your Operations Bible

This is not a difficult task, just a laborious one. You'll know everything your business does, so document it all the way you want it to be done. And that's it.

Start with the basics. Put yourself into a worker's shoes and complete a task, then write down how you did it. For example, if you answer the phone, script what you said and create a flow chart of what happened after the call. Take another call and flow chart what happens in this one.

Then read an email. Document how you want it answered and what the follow up process should be. Every day add more to your bible, and in time you'll have a fully understandable script of your business.

One of my favourite analogies for a business running at excellence is a theatre company performing the same show each night. Talented actors (the team) consistently deliver a stellar show that's been born from a script with instructions for backstage, sound and lighting. Any actor can learn the script and fill in should another actor leave. In fact, anyone can fill in should anyone else leave. Our Operations Bible will be our script for our show, the secret to a great business.

If you're thinking of starting out, I strongly recommended looking at 'legally scripted operated' businesses (I have made that phrase up). Some businesses must be audited by third parties, maybe a government organisation, in order to be legal to operate, for example an accountancy practice, a care home or anything medical. My nursery childcare business springs to mind here, and I'm in love with the concept. I didn't used to be but I am now, and here's why.

My nursery business's operating system came from a highly regulated, audited, inspected government framework. Heck, the government even supplies free training to meet the framework they require. This means three things:

- Competitors can't cut corners and degrade the industry – the government won't allow them to operate

- Low barrier to entry entrepreneurs can't disrupt the sector, so these businesses have much more sustainable value

- Banks and investors like the industry so it's far easier to sell the businesses on because they are consistent if run well.

Swipe some of these points into your business. Customers stay with a nursery business because they know it's consistently audited. Pretend that is the case for your business and the value will be huge. Businesses that do this well enter the world of franchising their brand and operating system – a well-known phrase when I first got into business was 'The fastest way to becoming a millionaire is to buy a McDonald's franchise'.

That's right. People pay a huge amount for an instruction kit and permission to use it.

Brand Bible

Another great thing to do as early as you can is to create your Brand Guidelines Bible, no matter what size your business is. It will clarify the personality the business has and deter you, the owner, from flitting between being an experience-led and a price-led business. This is undoubtedly a vision-based project and should have the input of entrepreneur and senior management.

The task doesn't have to be daunting. Imagine you are writing to someone you know; write with a cuddle and passion, and this will flow through the words.

Start your book of guidelines with a paragraph such as: 'We

are an Experience Business that never flits from our hard-earned brand rules. Your support and desire to share and enthuse them is our lifeblood. We want to be the best, and can only do this with your help.'

Then it's time for you to enter your rules, for example:

- What's your branding?

- What's your personality?

- What are your price rules?

- What are your colours?

- What are your views on xyz?

- What's a no-no? This could be 'We never discount'; 'We never supply this type of customer'; etc.

- What imagery would you use to describe your business in marketing?

- How do you write to your customers – professionally or quirkily?

- If your brand was a famous person, who would they be?

The last point is a good tactic to make your team understand what you want to achieve. I noticed a visitor attraction describe its business as Mary Wonka – half Mary Poppins, caring and disciplined with an element of fun, and half Willy Wonka for a touch of quirkiness.

Building your Brand Bible will keep the business owner focused and the team on point.

History is littered with companies that have flitted and never got back on track. Premium brands that price accordingly stand the test of time. As I write these words, I can think of tons of Experience Businesses that have lasted – Harrods, John Lewis, Selfridges – and I can't think of a single price-led one. When you compete on experience, you're building a brand for generations to use; when you compete on price, you need to get in, make your money and get out before the market gets you out. It's not for me. I chose legacy.

When you flit, your brand is damaged – fact. You must stay on course. If you have flitted then do all you can to get back on the track of long-term brand building rather than short-term survival. Don't panic if you have flitted. Learn from it. It's now time to keep to your Brand Bible rules. You may take a dip in custom while the market tests your longevity, but once you're there, you'll always be the best.

CHAPTER 5

Build a Business on Testimonials

The business that says, 'Thank you' in an outstanding way is the business that lasts. But this needs to be done in a way that leaves customers in love with it.

Let's look at why to embrace the 'thank you' from a business perspective.

Marketing costs money. It just does. Testimonial marketing is a by-product of great service, and in many cases absolutely free. It's unlike any other marketing. It's hard to track all it does, but you know word of mouth is working its little booty off for your business when you do a good job. And it certainly works. Pretty much everyone has bought as a result of testimonials. They are far more effective than expensive marketing. They turn prospects into predetermined buyers rather than shoppers. Word of mouth is *the* way to build a sustainable, commercially profitable business.

Some business owners that I meet boast that they never need to spread the word about the enterprise they have worked so hard to build. They spurt lines such as 'We don't need to advertise because we are so busy.'

I say, 'Bugger off.'

If you have a word of mouth business, your job, as its owner, MD or toilet block cleaner, is to amplify your excellence to the world. Take advantage of your word of mouth asset. Even when you're totally and utterly over-booked or over-subscribed, this is still a seriously smart thing to do. Not only does it mean you can put your prices up and increase profitability, it means you can elevate your status to being 'famously' the best. Then you can price yourself on exclusivity and look to further the customer experience and profitability of the business.

Undoubtedly, the way to build this type of 'sold out' business is to share the story of the success you have had. Not yet sold out? Start as you mean to go on. If you're doing a great job looking after your customers, you'll turn them into fans. Over time, their word of mouth will trickle customers into your business.

My method, however, gets them pouring into my organisation – I remind my customers to share the experience they've had.

One of the ways I do this is to share the feedback they give me immediately, and then a few days later remind them that they used my company. The trick is to do this in such a way that it leaves them in awe of my amazing enterprise.

We can do this is using a mixture of modern technology and good old-fashioned stuff:

- Verbally say, 'Thank you'
- Send out a questionnaire
- Third party testimonial groups
- A phone call
- An email
- A written card.

Are you testimonial famous?

Testimonials drive business as surely as a cow eats grass. They increase sales and are the cornerstone of a business of repute. In a crowded marketplace, testimonials can be the difference between shoppers using you and using your competitor. Tell your team and your brain this.

The obvious thing to do is to ask customers to tell a friend of the great service they have had. This creates an organic pipeline of 'word on the street' testimonials. It's a slow burner, but by far the best way to advertise. Your job is to find a way to expedite the process. The fact is that no marketing works as well as testimonial marketing, so amplify it.

Delight your customers

Leave your customers delighted and you'll always be the leader in business. Leave them happy and you'll always compete.

Share this mantra with your team; explain the essence of your culture. If you truly wish to build a business that makes waves, gets remembered and turns mountains of customers into loyal fans, similar to those of a sport team, then you will need to move away from 'happy'.

Customers who are happy flit from one happiness provider to another. Those who are left delighted describe your organisation using words like 'amazing', 'excellent' and 'out of this world'. Then you will have created a marketer for your business, and you didn't even know you were doing it.

Some businesses have achieved this so well, people will pay a fortune just to use their brand. I do it. I'll pay six times more to wear a shirt that advertises a profitable business than the equivalent shirt produced by a company that doesn't advertise anything. The brand announces to the world, 'I've just paid a lot for this and I'm keen to share that.'

The highest accolade for a business is when people love its

brand so much they will share it and boast about it. They'll do anything to stay loyal to the brand.

This must be the goal of the Experience Business. Do such a great job that your customers become your marketing department. They'll tweet, post, write, share live video, all in a bid to tell their friends and followers just how proud they are to have given you money.

So amplify the process. Don't let it just happen organically; add some fertiliser by asking your customers to do the above.

Embrace your personality business

Don't be a 'one size fits all' organisation. Some won't like you, but the ones who do will love you.

Some people love rock music, but hate pop. There have always been niches and different audiences, and I have experienced my fair share of this in my companies. Good thing too. I want loyal, loving fans, right on board with what I and my companies do. People who like what we do are flitters; those who dislike us go elsewhere. In my opinion, if there aren't some people putting you down, you're not making enough of a difference.

It's a fact that people fall in love with their specific choices, from music to food, exercise to holidays, and the same is true for business. Being weird and wonderful and a little out there can prove an excellent tactic for building a loyal audience.

Aiming to be famous to a few is far more attainable for your business than aiming to be famous to the masses.

Earlier in this chapter I explained that testimonial marketing will set the wheels in motion for this process, which takes work and dedication. When your organisation becomes famous, even only to a few, people regard doing business with you as an experience. I can't count the amount of times I have seen friends on social media share their experience of eating in a loved restaurant or buying an expensive car or out of this world handbag – it's just what people do.

Here's a classic for you that proves my case. Every year when the kids go back to school, social media goes into a frenzy of statuses showing them dressed up in their cute little uniforms. But compare these two statuses:

- Joe starts school today

- Joe starts school today at Eton.

People love to share that they have got the big brand in their possession. They want you to know that they're using the best, the most expensive that they can get their hands on. Now Eton won't be for everyone, but everyone knows what it is. That's part of achieving the famous status.

When my first title business started out, I was the most outrageous, the loudest. I entertained all the family, not just the kids, but this was not everyone's cup of tea.

My competitors would even say, 'We don't do what Jimbo does. We don't take the mick out of the adults.'

I used to hate it! Why couldn't everyone love me? But I soon realised that my competitors were talking about me because I had made a stir, and this was good news.

The people who loved me were fiercely loyal. They didn't want the safe card; they wanted the out there, unique card, and they'd book two years in advance to get it. I was famous to a few. Even though I was just a kids' entertainer serving Essex and London, people used to stop me in supermarkets so their kids could take a photo.

People do the same now at Entrepreneurs' Network events. It amazes me how quickly the EN elevated the team and me to the position of celebrities – it just happened. We now work hard to make our members famous for their fantastic entrepreneurial achievements. It works brilliantly.

Build your business to have a personality that's remembered. It's so much better to be loved by a few than liked by many. It's what rock stars do well. It's what successful businesses do well too. It's what the Experience Business does.

The Memory Making Organisation

To build a sustainable Experience Business that leaves a lasting impression, you need your loyal fans need to be in awe of what you do. So occasionally shock them with outstanding moments, and it's so much easier to do this when you run a business with plenty of margin.

Many companies use this tactic.

Years ago, Aaron, the MD of Partyman, visited Las Vegas with his chums. The guilt of leaving his significant other must have played heavily on his mind, so he took himself off to the Gucci shop and purchased a little something for her.

By the time he got back to England, this was on his doormat:

Dear Mr Othman

We hope you enjoyed your stay here in Las Vegas, and your wife loves her present. It was our pleasure to help you here in Gucci and thank you for choosing us.

If we can ever be of service, I will personally be available.

Yours

The Manager

Gucci – Las Vegas

Aaron was chomping at the bit to tell me it was hand written. It was real, it was in the post, and it amazed him. He was in awe. He was shocked.

A compete-on-price business would look at how much that letter cost to send around the world and the return on invested time. This type of business will do all it can to protect its slither of margin, but Gucci has built a trusted and loved brand, and its margin will be huge. It can send a letter to England for whatever it costs and still be profitable.

I want to turn now to hotels. I have stayed in plenty over the years. I hate the things – I much prefer home, but of my thousands of nights away in hotels, I can only remember the ones that have shocked and awed me. And as you've probably guessed, they were the expensive ones.

I remember the hotels with amazing artwork, excellent concierge service, the best breakfasts. I remember my stay in experience hotels: chocolates on the bed and champagne on arrival. The ones that cover the bed in rose petals and design towels to look like escapees from the jungle. The ones that overlook the ocean; the ones where nothing was too much. I remember these because they shocked me with their experience.

The fact is when hotels charge between £220 and £500 a night for a room, they have margin to give back to the customer. This creates huge brand loyalty when the customer gets more than they paid for, which is the secret to running an Experience Business. How many people post about hotels they have stayed in on social media? They take a picture of the view and the bed and the welcome champers they receive and become mini-marketers.

So, let's suppose we spend an extra £20 in raw cost to deliver something amazing to our customers that they aren't expecting. As a result, they love us. That's fan creation. But if a hotel charges only £80 a night and shocks the customer with £20 worth of extras, it will be giving away 25% of its takings.

The power of the unusual in a usual world dictates shock and awe's effectiveness. When I was nine, I visited the small Greek island of Kalymnos with my family. I remember bits of the island – it's beautiful – but what I really remember is the lovely apartment we rented. On the day we arrived, the lady who owned the apartment proudly introduced herself with a platter of homemade Greek food as a welcome gift, taking time to explain how she'd made it and some of the history of the island. Although I was only nine, I was in awe. My dad couldn't believe it either – it was so unusual. By investing a little time, she punched more shock than a bottle of bubbly. Sometimes the effort of time and uniqueness far outweighs the big money stuff.

I'd now like to share examples of the things that I have done over the years to shock and awe my followers. This stuff may not have cost a fortune, but it made big impacts. And it's all easily delivered when margin is your friend.

Jimbo

Seasoned followers of mine will know that my working life started as a simple sole trader. I charged with huge margin and delivered an excellent service, going above and beyond. I loved the business so much that I wanted to give memorable experiences. I was, in effect, a master solopreneur.

I would bring along backdrops, amazing props, make it snow – heck, I even made the birthday child fly. But some of the most well-received things I did just involved giving a little extra unpaid time, staying later or arriving earlier.

Telephone calls in advance and after the service could also increase customer love. The initial call clearly defined the customer's needs and requirements. Then I'd follow up for no reason other than to see if the customer was fabulously in love with my business and to say thank you.

From the kick-off of Jimbo to this day, I, and now my team, have always started the week with advance booking calls, purely to check in with future fans and make sure they love what we are going to do.

I'm also a big fan of using the post. An amazing confirmation letter of service provided gets a big tick from me. If you sign up to a snazzy credit card, for example, you want to see what arrives – amazing. It's instant devotion to the brand – the start of unparalleled customer excellence.

Experience brands use traditional touchy-feely stuff to complement the emails and tech they send. Companies that compete on price will consider the cost of a stamp in the bottom line; the Experience Business will consider the value of brand love.

The Father Christmas Experience

Partyman successfully runs one of the UK's most expensive Christmas grottos. The event has been running for some years, and at the time of writing it's the most profitable thing we do in leisure for the fifteen days it operates. This is because it has the strongest brand loyalty, based on the fact we reward our customers with so many shock and awe moments. We can afford amazing staff to play the elves; we go over the top on uniforms, set and costumes; we let our imaginations run away with us and deliver – because we have margin. If it's possible and will add to the event, we do it, so the customers have the best time. It's so liberating not to have to count every penny.

Our boldest move was to give the children a gift that wasn't a toy. We built a surprise toy shop from which the children could choose anything they liked, and afterwards they got a Build-A-Bear gift from Father Christmas – double whammy. The kids loved it; they couldn't believe it. The parents couldn't believe it either.

All this helped build our amazing Christmas experience.

Entrepreneurs' Network

My more recent business is the one that has prompted me to help business owners. In turn, this has led to more talks, more writing, a whole new office and amazing team.

Entrepreneurs Network (EN) was born from me sharing my experience, tapping away on Facebook, giving my views on business and occasionally a video. The aim was to set up a one-to-many business coaching organisation.

People would see what I was about, which created members who wanted more. They'd then buy my book, come to a seminar or join the group. In turn, they'd soar to success.

At conception, I planned to build a business that would love every member and help them as much as it could. I knew that as EN grew, the costs would dilute with volume, so I set my stall out to give more than was expected, knowing the business was built around margin. I wanted members for life so developed a platform that would deliver just that. But I knew I had to shock and awe my customers to build a tribe; a clan; a following.

EN runs amazing events to this day. We choose to use the O2 in London and take over the cinema with the super comfy seats. That's right – a business seminar in an armchair. Lovely. Throw in amazing speakers and lunch, and we started building something pretty special.

The events lose money – big money, every time. But we can afford it through our membership. We choose to give away value in our events as a thank you to our members. We also offer unlimited access to phone support from our advisors, a portal of online videos and files. Our members get more than they pay for.

Send a book

Often I'll send great customers one of my books – signed, of course, to add a little love. The arrival of a book from the author on the doorstep is intended to send happy hormones whizzing round the customer's brain.

Be entertaining

If you can entertain people, they have an unlimited attention span.

Experience Businesses have a way of captivating their customers. The trick is to trigger emotions which keep your customers' attention on you and no one else; it's a clever little skill that many Experience Businesses do without realising it.

Entertaining people is key, and I don't mean in a song and dance way. Simple stuff can keep a mind active and on your business. The mistake a lot of companies make is to bore the hell out of people in a bid to be professional. You can be an entertaining professional; some university lecturers are, and they always get the best results from the students they teach. Engage your customers and do it in an entertaining way – they'll love you for it. The power of emotion has a profound effect on customer loyalty. The entertainment factor needs to flow through the company, allowing prospects to keep their attention on you.

I used to frequent a Spanish island in my early holiday years, and the highlight was the 'Helados Man'. He would ride around the town on an old bicycle, singing. His smile was bigger than anyone else's and his demeanour was entertaining. He sold to an audience that loved him, and even though he charged three times more for his ice cream than anyone else, his queues were always the longest.

This same island had a square of restaurants. All were busy, but one particular one was always overbooked. Why? Because the front of house manager communicated by whistling. Customers, waiters and kids all loved it. It wasn't about price; people went to the restaurant to be entertained.

If you as a company can strike a chord of emotion with your prospects, you'll find them so much more loyal to you. They'll love you for who you are. Have a read of your website, check your last video and see if it keeps you engaged and entertained to the end, then ask someone else what they think. It's a crowded market in business and it's getting more and more crowded every year, so the trick is to be entertaining and you'll have a business that gets noticed.

I speak a lot about business, usually at boring seminars where the audience has switched off. I believe my content is good, but if they ain't listening to me, what the hell does it matter? My first tactic is to entertain my audience. I'll shock them with a huge hello and energy, and I have seen others start their talk by having a go at someone in the audience. Both tactics break state and engage an audience.

Learn how to write entertaining copy and memorable social media posts, and make engaging videos. There's an entertainer in all of us.

Change with the times

But don't change the company's personality. Involve the whole team and listen to ideas from all levels.

Times change, folks. They always will, but many traditionalists who own businesses fight change with everything they have. The fact is simple: embrace change in order to survive. No ship is too big to avoid the iceberg. But there is a skill to keeping the business's personality while changing the way it moves forward.

Steve Jobs is a classic example.

Steve spent some time away from Apple. During his sabbatical, the company lost its way and didn't move with the times, hoping to rely on its generic personality alone. When Steve returned, he spiced it all up, innovated and injected his own personality, but kept the higher price, higher end ethos. I'm sure you don't need me to tell you how it all panned out for him and Apple.

Customer cuddles

The Experience Business allows you to invest in your customers. If you're at the stage of giving customer 'cuddles', they will speed up the process of turning customers into fans who'll love you. Giving customer cuddles means giving them regular one to one attention, making them feel like they're the only one.

The customer cuddle is quite possibly the best marketing you'll do. Get it right and you'll make some serious fans of your business who will tell the world about you.

The process of turning a prospect into a fan is this:

- Prospect

- Shopper

- Customer

- Happy customer

- Advocate

- Fan

And with customer cuddles, you can remove the middle stages.

The process works best when the whole team is empowered to give customer cuddles. The purpose of a customer cuddle is to make the business seem affectionate and loving. Training this culture is something that must come from the top down.

Outside business, a cuddle is shared between two people who know and love each other. Having a bad day? Would a cuddle help? A crying child can quickly be pacified with a cuddle.

The dictionary says a cuddle is to '*Hold close in one's arms as a way of showing love or affection*'. Now I have actually cuddled customers in my business, and many of them have cuddled me. This is because my team and I have gone over and above, and those customers absolutely love us.

Customer cuddles can be as simple as using a customer's name, bending the rules to help a customer or offering something that isn't the norm.

My old man was a sparky. We used to trundle down to the local electrical wholesaler, and I loved going there as a kid because the man who owned it had a giant pot of lollypops.

He'd always invite me to choose one from the pot with a smile and a pat on the head. Three decades on, I still remember this.

It takes a lot for a kid to beg his dad to take him to the wholesalers.

Surprise and delight customers. Turn them into fans – it's the way an Experience Business with margin survives.

CHAPTER 7
Amazing Aesthetics

The look and feel. The set.

Without a doubt, an amazing environment is essential to create an outstanding business, even more so for one that sets its stall out to compete on experience, but only when the human element is in place first. Humans can create a story that enthuses the brain, just like the theatre production we spoke about in Chapter 6. Then your company's look and feel complement what's real, and you'll be winning extra marks in the customer's mind along the way.

So let's talk set. We have the human element in place and we are now in the process of touching up the finer details, just as brand leaders like Apple and Disney do so well. For example, now's when a fine dining restaurant will source the best carpets, scents and light bulbs to get the ambience just how they want it.

A friend of mine, Matt Mason, who helped me in my early days with super advice, gets it. He has an eye for what the customer sees; he understands the importance of the set. In a recent conversation, he was harping on about how he rips all the grass and flower beds up at his exceptional wedding venue so the flowers get the right amount of water to look glorious all year long, and the water drains from the grass on wet days. It's this attention to detail that makes Matt Mason a clear player in the Experience Business.

Look and feel are back of mind in most cases. No one talks about them if they're good, but if they're outstanding, people will. Aim to make yours so excellent that people want to take a photo and share it with the world. But if the look and feel are bad, customers will also want to talk about them and take a photo to share, but for the wrong reason.

A classic example is a clean carpet in a hotel. It doesn't get noticed. But a smelly, sticky carpet will be very noticed. Mr and Mrs Back Of Mind will not be pleased. However, a red carpet with gold barriers and red ropes will also be noticed, and not just by Mr and Mrs Back Of Mind. Mr and Mrs Conscious will take note too.

Waterfalls in reception, perfumed rooms, natural lighting, music and furniture in waiting areas all pack a punch in amazing aesthetics. The trick is to bring it all to the attention of the conscious mind.

Outstanding theme parks play upbeat music. On arrival, guests are greeted by huge welcome signs and flower beds before they've even got inside the park. This sets the tone. Disney builds a flower bed in the shape of Mickey Mouse, creating the 'must take photo' moment. Hell, they even built a castle as a backdrop.

Of course, this all costs, so you need to have a healthy margin. So many business owners try to add expensive stuff when the margin doesn't allow it – you need meat on the bone. Start with the small things. A great selling trick for bakeries, for example, is to pump the smell of cooking into the shop. The set, the look and, in this case, the scent of baking create the desire. Customers relate the smell to a happy experience and then buy.

To understand the elements of set, check out my diagram, the Star of Set Excellence.

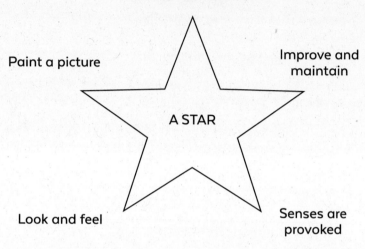

The Eye

Audit and organise

Paint a picture

Improve and
maintain

A STAR

Look and feel

Senses are
provoked

The eye

You need to have an all-seeing eye, an eye for detail, even if the thing you see is nothing to do with your department. If Julie in Accounts notices an overflowing bin or a dirty car park, she will still report it.

Management must have an eye for what looks good and take action on anything that's not right. This sounds obvious, but it's quite a talent to notice detail on a regular basis and action improvements.

Audit and organise. If the eye for detail notices problems, like a regularly messy area, the management systemises to mitigate it happening again.

The business must be organised to maintain a well-polished set that customers see and employees work in. The 'backstage' of the business needs to be as clean and tidy as the front, for it's back of house that allows the front to work. For example, a well-organised kitchen means that the restaurant staff can perform their duties easily.

A regular check of what's on show is the way to run the business efficiently.

Paint a picture. Everything should form a story in your set, even if you run a dentist surgery, estate agent or care home.

Imagine you're telling a story in your set design when customers interact with your business. Stories are the easiest way to hammer home the vision. For an estate agent, this could mean having calm, welcoming offices, creating a professional home from home environment.

Paint a picture in your mind's eye of what the office should look like. Then get ready to set it up and take a picture of the final article. If the real picture looks as good as the one in your mind's eye, you've succeeded.

I've spent a lot of money creating sets over the years, all to enhance the experience for my guests and make my story feel as real as possible. The sets have played a big part in assisting my team members do a better job.

If your team believe in the set, so will your customers.

Look and feel. These are important. Make sure the set looks and feels great, as this can have a huge impact on the behaviour of your team members and customers (fans).

I have been to many a meeting in offices around London, so I have seen how excellent workplaces make people proud and boost productivity. These offices have instantly made me think more of the business, and the same is true of theme parks, shops, restaurants, and even warehouses. The Scrooge in me wants to believe this is a waste of money, but it's not. When your company can afford it, invest in every area of the business to create a positive look and feel.

Improve and maintain. I spend a colossal amount of cash every year maintaining and improving the sites and businesses I own and operate, but frankly, I don't spend enough. I'm constantly driving cash into making them the best they can be. I employ a whole team to paint, decorate and build. I look to improve all we do, all the time.

The Experience Business never gives up on a continuous improvement plan. Be ready to invest a chunky amount back into the business to keep it looking fresh.

Senses are provoked. The aim of the Experience Business is to provoke all the senses – a beautiful sight for the eyes; the perfect sound accompanying what the eyes see; the correct smell; the right warmth.

Every sense must be provoked for the right reason. An amazing set can so easily go wrong. Picture a beautiful day nursery with cash, gardens, facilities, toys and airy rooms. Parents can't wait to enrol their children. Then put in a member of staff with a dirty uniform, scruffy hair and chewing gum, and leave rubbish flowing out of the bins. The parents will soon think that the place is not that great after all.

A fine dining restaurant that plays the wrong genre of music too loud and has a dirty waiter with BO – disaster in no time, with just a few simple things out of place.

Investment into creating beautiful work environments fosters a strong culture within the team that will translate to the customer side. When you can afford it, do it.

CHAPTER 8

Be the Ultimate Expert

Predetermination, the Holy Grail of the Experience Business, is what happens when people choose your brand. They walk into their favourite designer shop knowingly, predetermined, ready to act. Ultimately, this is buying from the experts.

If someone is ill, they'll almost certainly act on the doctor's advice because he or she is the expert. Got toothache? Likelihood is you'll consult your dentist. People on the whole are predetermined to act in these situations, whatever the cost. It's the power experts have.

Experts deliver the ultimate experience and earn trust. They are always expensive and rarely questioned. In any industry where consumers choose to do business for a special reason, they choose the experts. But to my shock and horror, some businesses don't set themselves up to be the experts. Maybe they don't feel they are worthy. If that's the case, they will always compete on price.

Being perceived as the expert is as important as *being* the expert. You need to shout about your expert status and build on it. But some experts are useless at letting people know.

Then there are charlatans who are great at being perceived as the experts. People will be conned till the end of time by nasty bastards ripping them off with fake expertise. But here's the thing that the charlatans have over the real experts: the ability to market themselves, and they create sales on the back of this. So if you fail to market yourself as the expert, you'll fail in getting the customer who's looking for you and is willing to pay, whatever the price.

So if you really believe you are the expert, tell the world that very thing. All industries have expert brands and expert thought leaders. They started from zero, and so can you.

To find out more about the all-important section of super-success that's sales and marketing, get in touch with the Entrepreneurs' Network (hello@entrepreneurs-network.co.uk). We have a shed load of expertise and resources to help you.

Based on my own experience of building expert credibility, I've put together some stories to help you deploy my tactics.

Write a book

This is my second book on business, and I have a pipeline of titles on the way. I'm not a natural writer; I really have to push myself to do it. But the feeling of satisfaction on the arrival of my book is special. Joe Public respects writers, which naturally creates trust.

Authors get profile. For this reason, writing a book is worthy of your time and effort when you're creating predetermination in prospects. My first book led to me meeting some great people and opened up lots of doors. I gave interviews, got speaking opportunities and clients, and gained new followers for the Entrepreneurs' Network.

Writing books and articles takes time, and it's not for the money they make. It's for the position they allow you to have. You become an *authority* in your field. And you don't have to kick off with a book. LinkedIn articles, blogs and emails sharing your thoughts, consistently and regularly, will elevate you and position you.

Speaking

Public speaking works like nothing else, especially if you share the stage with other experts and well-known individuals. It's really powerful when you become good at it – practice makes perfect.

I can remember signing 120 members to the Entrepreneurs'

Network on the back of a 60-minute talk. It also allowed me to meet other great speakers and form new partnerships.

For me, getting up on stage come easily. I love it. Most people, though, have a fear of being on stage. It takes time to overcome the fear and feel confident.

Polish your pitch and elevate your expertise. It'll do wonders for you, and create instant fans it would have taken years to find via traditional business methods.

Industry awards

A well-respected business takes a long time to build, and speeding the process up comes from expertise. Rarely is an entrepreneur's success an overnight story.

Awards showcase people whom others think well of. Try and win as many as possible, then tell the world. You'll get noticed, and may even attract other experts who want to work with you.

Marketing

It never ceases to amaze me how crappy most businesses' marketing is. My heart bleeds at how much money is wasted every day by awful marketing. I love seeing how EN members blossom into marketing once they implement the things my team teaches them. And one of these things is to be testimonial famous.

Got amazing awards or TripAdvisor reviews that say you're fantastic? Then tell people in your marketing. As a little pressie, my team of amazing marketers will review your marketing for free to see if you're on point.

Just email hello@entrepreneurs-network.co.uk and let us know how we can help.

Endorsement

Big companies or well-known organisations endorsing you is super-powerful.

In the early days of my career, I would do free shows for schools and nurseries. The school brand endorsed me by booking me, then the parents booked me.

Fast forward a decade, Partyman and its group of companies get asked to work with smaller companies to help elevate them. People ask EN on a daily basis if they can speak at our events or formulate partnerships. They know our brand holds sway as an endorsement.

If you have some high profile clients and you're allowed to say you work with them, put that into your pitch. I tend to find others follow when you do that. Seek brand endorsement, and when you become a heavyweight, be ready for people to ask you to endorse them.

Fame

Celebrity status will elevate you, and becoming famous is not so difficult. Well, not as difficult as you might think. You just need to work at it.

Becoming famous to a few is easy. It's a question of effort, marketing and doing a good job. Being famous to the masses takes more hard work and scaling up. Start with small articles, speaking events and awards. Then pitch to TV companies about making a documentary of your business. Think about how you can be branded as 'famous for....'.

The Experience Business is known to be the best, and using yourself, the Founder, as a marketable asset is smart. Are you a personality who could do that well? If that's not you, then make the business famous. My tactic would be to do both, but just the business is fine if you're not the celebrity type.

Growing the empire

We grow a business within a business empire by folding it into an existing empire. Smart Experience Businesses lend their trusted brand to lower priced items that provide residual sales rather than one-off highly profitable sales. This is thinking I often practise.

If you build an amazing Experience Business, you too can benefit from this. It's like gaining little house points of appreciation from your customers so you can sell them a commodity item with an increased margin. It's your reward. I find it's far easier to use an experience brand to sell a commodity item with a bigger margin than it would be for a commodity business to sell an experience-based brand.

Imagine Rolex deciding to start selling towels – an everyday item, but Rolex could sell them for double the normal price. They could lend their brand to anything to get more regular sales, like Ferrari has done with fashion, and now theme parks in Spain and Dubai.

And this can be 100% emulated by an SME, giving it a real chance to increase margins and prices on what would be otherwise 'commoditised' products. The price is never questioned because of the backing of the experience brand.

I worked with a florist member of the Entrepreneurs' Network. They were known, liked and trusted in the area they served, mainly for creating amazing flower displays for events. On the back of that business, they sold chocolates and greeting cards at huge margins, but the price was hardly questioned because they successfully ran an Experience Business. They went on to build another florist, creating an empire on the back of one Experience Business with the Wow Factor.

The big boys have nailed the concept too. Only the super-rich can stay in the best hotels every night of the week. People don't visit Disney World every day, nor do they fly first class often. Are people going to buy a new phone, Mac or iPad each week? No, they're biannual sales at most, but Apple sells music all the time through iTunes. So the smart idea for businesses is to get their flock to buy regular items at a higher price than the competition. Disney toys, for example, are double the price of their unbranded cousins. In essence, this keeps the cash flowing and the business going.

Fact is, smart businesses use their brands to build a web of wow lifetime experiences that allow them to charge premium prices for day to day products. I have been doing this from the day I started in business. When my life as an entrepreneur kicked off, I was a one sale a year company. People don't hire entertainers every week. I was desperate to change this, so I increased the company's income by starting an agency and charging other entertainers a fee for referrals. But the real trick came when I added other services to my company, using my Experience Business to sell normal stuff without having to compete with the price-led boys. I hired inflatables and face painters out and sold party bags, all at increased prices. Customers were buying *Jimbo* party bags; my flock had bought into my experience brand.

Fast forward to the present day, and as an owner of leisure destinations, I've done the same thing again. Commodity items sell at prices that carry a margin. Yes, an ice cream will cost more than one from a supermarket because it befits the experience guests have.

This is what the Experience Business allows you to do.

CHAPTER 9

Good to Great

The profitable Experience Business's secret weapon is a diverse team of entrepreneur, management and thinkers. My key formula in running all types of companies is:

Entrepreneurship + Management = Success

I believe a company needs strong leadership and vision setting (objectives) from the entrepreneur, and management to make them happen. If it's right, it's an amazing partnership. I am so lucky to have this in the companies I am part of. But running an Experience Business is as much about passion as it is about profit. The passion for excellence and continuous improvement only happens on the back of loving the beast you own. Looking at the world's most successful companies, we can see they are all the products of a passionate individual who didn't give up.

The hard truth is this: if you are not passionate about your business, you won't hit the big time. Non-stop thinking, never giving up and making the impossible possible are all traits of the passionate individual. You have to be hungry. If you're not hungry for success and passionate enough to feed that hunger, the business is not for you.

Experience Businesses take a lot of dedication. They're the long game; the high barrier to entry; the envy of the competition. They have passionate customers who never look elsewhere; who love and expect excellence. And the love of a passionate customer starts with a passionate Founder.

As I write this, I find myself thinking about all the companies I run, and all the things I need to do to make them better. Nothing is ever good enough for me; I strive to do better, be better, and frown on the points that need more work. I am the dad who walks around Disney World with a little tear, knowing that Walt would never see just how much his passion paid off. His legacy paved the way for an Experience Business that's going to live for centuries.

With passion, you get dedication, and this is the only way you'll keep going through the inevitable setbacks all companies have. When you start thinking outside the box, it's far harder to get followers. But followers are essential to help feed your hunger. My early followers, in the form of team members, bank managers, partners, landlords and anyone else who bought into my vision, helped underpin my success.

Vision is the key word here. Those who have seen me speak at conferences and events will know I go on and on about how a powerful vision can attract followers to an organisation. Share where you want to go and watch your followers parade your passion on their sleeves. These followers must be loved and cherished – a small handful of mega-passionate people can be the secret behind an outstanding company.

If you want to build an amazing company, understand that shit happens. The bigger your vision, the harder it'll be getting there, but when you're there, you'll love it. Experience Businesses are the result of passion and hard work. They're far easier to achieve if you love what you're doing.

Tiny improvements add up

Earlier we spoke about building a company that delights customers and turns them into fans. Imagine the power your business will have when it reaches this status. So in real terms, you need to move your business from good to great.

To scale a great company is so much harder than to scale a good company. I learned this phrase from a friend and mentor, Andrew Wolfe, who also says, 'Excellent is the enemy of the very good.' It's far better to start building the whole company to be very good than some parts average and one part excellent. The journey to excellence, once the very good stage is established, is met when a business polishes every detail in tiny increments. Improving a business by 1% every day consistently will have 100% improvements in place in a little over a quarter.

If you are like me and run a multi-site operation over a large geographical patch, then your focus needs to be very good all round driven by a system that promotes continuous improvement. If, however, you're a smaller beast, then excellence is far easier to achieve. This is not to say excellence cannot be achieved at a larger level, but the investment will be so much more in terms of time, money and resources.

Here's a clear-cut example. In this case, I want to focus on greeting people.

A good company's team will answer the phone like this: 'Hallo, Entrepreneurs' Network,' with an average tone and welcoming manner and a degree of company understanding.

A great company will answer the phone like this: 'Good afternoon, Entrepreneurs' Network, Davina speaking. How can I help you today? May I take your name?'

The team member using their own name, asking for the customer's name and offering to help are all little improvements that add up to making the customer fizz inside. In our example, Davina is starting to turn a prospect into a happy customer, and maybe even a fan. The phrase I bat about is 'Being 10% better turns you from a good company to a great company, average to good.'

In my experience of running my own large companies and mentoring lots of others, I've seen that the struggle to meet customers' demand for excellence comes down to a lack of educating the team on what the company vision is. When I buy businesses, impressing my culture on team members with bad habits is difficult, especially when there are a lot of them. Regularly updating my plans and vision will win the day in most cases.

My favourite way to do this is to build a quick-fire culture statement that's continually shared, especially when people start in the company. Heaven knows, new recruits without the proper training can cost you dearly. Even when you have people working for you seasonally, you still need a way to maintain standards.

With this a constant battle, I developed an idea called the 4 Es. They can be adapted for any company.

At Partyman, the culture standards that drive us are to be:

- Entertaining

- Enthusiastic

- Engaging

- An experience.

These quick guidelines cover our beliefs. Everything else builds from these.

The people you employ will be a large factor in making a good company, and the great companies will be full of people who are better than the Founder. Want great company? Get a great manager. Can't find a great manager? Ask yourself whether you are allowing one in. Great companies cannot survive on management alone, nor can they survive on entrepreneurship alone. Every day, seek to add value to the people who buy from, work for and interact with the company. A great company employs people who think this one thing: *How does this decision add value to my customer?*

To kick start the process, look for daily improvements. Every business can make a 1% improvement on a daily basis. They'll soon add up, and they don't always have to cost money.

CHAPTER 10

Market by Attraction

The simple fact is that some businesses need to market hard and some need to remind the flock to buy, but all businesses need to market.

What an Experience Business does is train its customers to buy. It attracts them and pulls them towards it by being the best. The Experience Business never pushes, never discounts, as it doesn't need to. It may have offers to drive loyalty and increase profit and margins further, but these will never be to attract customers.

This is a key difference between the Experience Business and a price-led business. The former looks to increase average customer value while the latter looks to drive the number of customers and feed the monster with any sales possible. The Experience Business has a customer avatar. It knows the customers it wants; it wants quality, not quantity.

I think now of Ferrari, a quality brand that understands exactly who its customers are. Ferrari has trained its customers to wait for the cars, not just expect the cars. So much so that Ferraris now sell for more second hand than they do new. This attracts people to act. No pushing here – Ferrari pulls customers towards its way of doing business on its terms.

This is the way an Experience Business operates. Its marketing is purely to advise and tell the fans what's next, whereas other businesses market in a way that calls people to action now. The call to action in an Experience Business is merely to remind customers that if they hesitate, they may miss out.

In my Christmas grotto business, I experience just this. If customers don't take action straight away then they won't get in. The marketing I now use is simply to remind people I'm open for business. I also let people know when it's sold out to promote word of mouth.

When building an Experience Business that stands the test of time, survival tactics can kick in at first – God knows, I have used discounting to attract cash. The trick is to move away from this short-term thinking as soon as you can.

Super brands never compromise their brand guidelines. You will never find cheap deals to get into Disney World. You'll never find big designer labels allowing discounting on their branded products. If Ray-Ban, for example, allowed a 50% price reduction, for sure there would be a huge spike in sales, but the medium-term damage would be catastrophic. People would think Ray-Ban was less premium, which would tarnish its brand loyalty in the back of customers' minds.

I remember an optician selling Ray-Bans at cost as a way of bringing customers into his store. Smart move? No. Ray-Ban hated it and threatened to stop supplying the optician if he discounted their RRP. Years spent building a brand is not to be frittered away by competing on price.

And Experience Businesses do spend years building a brand that attracts loyalty, training customers to think that its service or product will never be compromised by price. Instead, they'll get the best experience and will love it, but they'll have to pay for it. Experience Businesses are the fillet steak of the industry they operate in; everyone else is a hamburger.

I worked with a boutique hotel chain which had built a sustainable business but needed to create some survival turnover. Before they had a customer base, they thought discounting was the answer. By 50%. No!

After speaking to them, I devised a plan to keep them competing on experience. Here's what we did.

We offered a bottle of Moet and welcome desserts on arrival if guests booked within the next seven days, complete with butler service and roses in the room. This headline offer had the punch of big discounting without degrading the product.

To get sales, the Experience Business markets itself to add value or exclusivity, not to discount.

Use technology to enhance relationships

In a world of technology, it can be so tempting to automate every little thing. Far better to use technology to enhance the experience rather than making it the entry to your business.

Nowadays, you'll find it unusual to have humans in place of a machine. Every decade, technology gets greater and the need for humans is reduced. This is fine and it works, but smart Experience Businesses compete using amazing customer service and then enhance the relationship via technology.

Recently Natalie and I flew to Greece for a little getaway and stayed in the best hotel. The team that ran the hotel competed on experience and they were outstanding. The poolside bar was hugely expensive, but was so cuddled in human interaction, it didn't matter.

But to get there, we had no choice but to use a budget airline. These guys competed so much on price that they'd do anything to remove human interaction. This was taken to new levels on check in – not a human in sight. We checked in via machine.

Let's look at being in love. When you meet the gorgeous someone in your life and can think of nothing else but them, you find yourself doing all you can to woo them, going out of your way to deliver the best experience of you possible. You can text the person, email them at work and call whenever you can – technology enhances the relationship, but it didn't create it.

Before anyone says, 'But I met my partner online and we're happy', the relationship only really started when you met up, proving you're real and human. It's how we work, people. If you create leads and contacts via technology, do all you can to make them as real as possible. Make the effort to meet people; this makes for great relationship building. It's so unusual for people to use the phone nowadays, a quick call will make you stand out, and that's the trick when competing on experience.

Rule of thumb: never ask for sex on the first date! Build and forge your relationships. Your partner will love a random text telling them how much you miss them, and the same tactic works for business relationships. Court your customer, then keep in touch – and that's where technology can come in handy.

CHAPTER 11

Educate

Folks, mainly other business owners, have often said to me, 'Wow, your team is amazing! You must pay them a fortune.' But my companies are like any other on pay – no more than usual. Our superpower in doing better than most is that we have a clear vision of what good looks like, what excellent looks like, and how to share this in an entertaining, educating way with our team members.

We know the step by step process to success. Sure, it's time and embedded practice, but the magic starts before team members even set foot inside the company.

The more famous your company is for being amazing, the more top people will want to work for it. They have been in effect educated as a consumer by the company's success.

Working in an Apple store is an example. The team members are all massive Apple fans before they work there, which will make them predetermined to want to work for Apple. Their passion for the product, their belief in the brand, then rubs off on consumers.

I remember buying a MacBook Air and listening to the sales guy tell me, 'it's a thing of beauty.' It's this vision, taught to the team, that naturally flows through them. To do the same in your company, start this from the ground up.

Don't get me wrong, my companies have had the polar opposite of this too. We are guilty of having some bad eggs in our ranks. The more you delegate, the less control you'll have. If you try to grow too fast, it can lead to panic employment, and that will be your biggest flaw. You can't delegate without first having a system in place. The process of excellence is a process.

The best schools take the best students who want to make something of their lives. They have the right attitude and want to be educated. This gives the school a head-start in shooting up the 'league tables of excellence'. Then when the students go home, their parents are pushing them to do well at school too, compounding their success.

It's the same for smart businesses. Success surrounds itself with success and breeds more success – continually raising the bar. Some people have the best attitudes; they're ready to learn. It's your job to take these students, educate them and skill them up. Look for happy, hard-working people with willingness to be educated on the way *you* want your company to be.

Once you have found your talent you need to start educating.

First, educate daily for excellence. I prefer the word 'educate' to training, but it is training the team to be the best that creates excellence. To guide your teams to success as an organisation, train them more and more.

Imagine spending twenty minutes a day training each individual who works for your company. What would that do for your company's productivity? Imagine how empowered the employees would feel to have twenty minutes of training dedicated to them, every morning before the work day starts. Heck, even just ten minutes!

In most companies, people are trained heavily on the day or week they start, maybe shadowing another average employee who demonstrates their interpretation of how things work. Continuous training is then done either in fits and starts and or when things go wrong.

At Partyman, we call this 'fire fighter' training. Companies will often parachute the owners or best team members in to manage the 'fires' the company itself has caused. But these fires can nearly always can be prevented by systems and processes and regular training.

Organise a well-structured training programme to occur as regularly as humans need to eat or drink. The business needs efficient and regular training. Ten minutes a day will train your team for a business that will survive; twenty minutes will train them for a business that will excel and lead the way.

Training's a never-ending story. Here are seven top tips that can be implemented easily to move things forward with little cost.

Create a vision, mission and culture statement. Vision is the life plan of the company, mission is how to deliver the vision, culture is what the team looks and acts like to action this.

Remind your team regularly of the above through daily training and social media groups. Social media is where people spend their time, it's instant and it's accessible. My companies use secret Facebook groups and emails to remind our team of our culture.

Mystery Shop. Solicit the help of either mystery shoppers or outsiders who will be honest about their views of your company. You need this.

You're not allowed to hand pick who does the mystery shopping. Do it when your business is most vulnerable or busy to get the best and most honest feedback possible. This will give you the oomph to improve.

Things get missed when you see them every day. A fresh pair of eyes could be the best training for the team and management of your enterprise.

We have had team members quite upset about results from mystery shops. One manager nearly cried, which proved they cared at least. The results have caused some massive positive changes, as the mystery shop feedback comes from the horse's mouth – the public. It can't be ignored.

If you think a mystery shop could be good for your business, email my team at EN (hello@entrepreneurs-network.co.uk). We can help you organise this.

Company language. There's no getting away from it, folks, you need to create your own language to be successful. (I put that line in for giggles. You don't really.)

The truth is, you'll know you're on the way when a language starts to be created by osmosis. If this happens in your company, give yourself a high five. This is good news, so amplify it.

My Entrepreneurs' Network co-founder, Mark Creaser, is a smart fellow. He calls this 'proprietary' language.

In effect, if your team members say things that will only be understood by others in the know, they form a special clique, and people like that. It creates a sense of belonging, safety, familiarity and contentment – all trademarks of the Experience Business.

For example, if I say Big Mac, people think McDonald's. If I say iPad, people think Apple.

Organisations, religions, families, schools all have words or phrases that only mean things to them and the people who follow them. My nan always used to call the remote control for the TV the 'zapper', and only the family knew what she meant. At Partyman, we call parties 'wowwees' and describe excellent as 'fabadousa'. We sign our emails off with 'Magically yours'. Internally, we have management and operating terms that will take a while to learn, but once new team members know the terms, they come close to the action.

I love the fact that members of the Entrepreneurs' Network are brought closer to each other by understanding the proprietary language we use. I love it even more when they teach rookies the meaning instead of me or my team having to do it. That's magic. That's an achievement.

So, if your company's proprietary language is already developing by osmosis, what would happen if you amplified it a little? The use of your own unique words to describe something is a good thing.

The importance of setting. A tidy, organised setting enhances productivity and culture. When the 'backstage' looks messy, your team is likely to allow messiness to continue. Allowing deliveries to be left in reception for five minutes means quite simply you allow standards to slip for five minutes.

The business is a stage, the team members are the actors, the management the directors. The entrepreneur provides the script and the story. Follow the story in the education of the team.

Go undercover as a customer. This is my favourite tactic for seeing boo-boos in the business. Regularly I don civilian clothing and visit my companies as a customer. I call up the call centre and pretend to book a party. I listen to conversations in the restaurants, watch the shows, queue up and look at the flows that my customers go through.

My senior team does it too. We use our learning from it to polish our training systems – what works now may not work forever.

Morning and afternoon meetings. This takes a lot of discipline and has to be done daily to become quick and efficient.

Irregular staff meetings do not educate or enhance communication. If team meetings are sporadic at best, then to the team they are a fact-finding, information-giving exercise. Of course, some meetings are better than none, whatever business you run, but if you only do them occasionally, either people are too scared at first to answer any questions, or they ask so many that the meeting goes off point and nothing gets done.

I am a massive fan of a two to ten-minute daily meeting that all team members come along to. It creates a culture of education and irons out problems. The meetings become super quick if they're regular, and the impact is huge. You get to educate your team daily, and the team gets to tell you what changes are needed to be a better business. Finally, you have a team all paddling in one direction.

Can't manage daily? At least hold them weekly.

Go to the competition. Invest time in meeting other business owners, and go undercover too. Take your team to the market leaders, show them what's possible and show them what's bad.

My biggest business decisions and ideas have come from seeing what others do. I have spent thousands of pounds travelling so my team can see what the competition does, and how in many cases we can put our spin on it to do it better. We do this every month, and sometimes more often. After all, the Experience Business needs to experience other businesses to educate itself.

Survey, baby, survey

Comment cards as regular as smiles, thank you calls as common as air, follow-ups as routine as cups of tea.

You need to know customers' 'back of mind' thinking to build an Experience Business. This is tough stuff to find out, but comments like 'We had a great day, but it didn't snow for long enough' are the gems you are looking for.

The Christmas Experience takes up a big bulk of my time. It fits so many of the rules for the Experience Business – it's got margin, magic and marvellousness. We obsess over the set, the outfits, the cast members – all of it, making the characters look like they've just stepped out of Lapland.

It was obsession that made us build doors at elf height – children loved the idea of walking where the elves went. Obsession made us pump the smell of freshly baked cookies into the attraction, this detail drove the experience to the max, and we continue to do more and more every year to improve further.

In this business we strived to exceed expectations. When margin allows we obsess over detail through continual nit picking and make tiny little improvements that have a big impact on our guests.

A classic example of this was thrown my way in the form of a recent customer comment.

One of the attractions on Partyman's Father Christmas Experience is to meet 'Flake', who's a live elf making snow using his 'Snowsaphone' (a lit-up saxophone). He does this with the help of invisible elves only Father Christmas can see. The guests participate with snow shakers and magic to make it snow, which it does. This all happens in a forest-themed setting twinkling with lights, and our guests love it.

However, a loyal visitor noticed that we did a great build up, but the actual snowing part didn't last long enough.

Over the years, I've found one of my customers' biggest gripes is queuing for stuff. At Partyman, we work really hard to lose the little cretins called queues, and the way we do it is to control our customers and think for them.

More and more smart businesses are systemising customers after conducting surveys and reviewing customer flow in their organisations. The way to achieve this is to harness the power around you. Technology has helped massively, researching competition will catapult you, and acting as if you're a customer will make you swing. Each of these three points moves the Experience Business along, but the last point is the most important. You need to experience what your customer experiences. You need to *be* the survey.

To deliver excellence to the customer, you need a ton of life experience. If you don't have experience, you are just a theory person. So survey what works and what doesn't, and understand the customers' desires. Then deliver those desires in a manageable way.

My first leap into running a high price experience was a Christmas grotto. I had all the theory in a cocktail I had conjured up. Guests would arrive at the post office, hop on a train, immerse themselves in the journey and meet the conductor, then arrive at Santa's station. The children would meet Santa and make a teddy to take home. After that, the experience continued with the chance to do some Christmas crafts and meet Mother Christmas.

I got the set right, I got the location right, I had the theory, but I had zero experience. Customers turned up whenever they liked and would all go to one place and cause bottlenecks. We had three hour waits, we ran out of stuff and the team members were stressed.

I reviewed all the complaints after the first year, spoke to customers and surveyed what we needed to do. Technology helped, as it allowed me to channel customers by timing their arrival and see when we needed to staff up or down.

My team and I know most of the competition in the sectors we operate in. This became particularly powerful when I scripted the new Christmas Experience. I looked at other theme parks and noticed how the customers flowed from one attraction to another in groups, led by actors. They never felt like they had to queue, so I swiped this technique and made it fit my jolly Christmas offering.

Finally, I dressed as a member of the public and became a customer of my and other people's businesses. This allowed me to hear and see first-hand what our flaws were. This experience of the business helped my team and me completely re-design the operation. We kept the elements that worked, but took control of the customer flow and guided them. We knew they didn't want to queue, we knew they wanted the experience to be more magical and intimate, so we delivered that in our own way.

Surveying customers can lead to little changes which add up to excellence. Often the changes cost nothing; things just need a rethink.

Success breeds success

The high barrier will only protect you for so long. Your competition will catch you up.

The devilish thing about business is there are always swine looking, seeking and seizing. These swine are called entrepreneurs – and I am one of them. Therefore, you need evolution in your business,

Earlier in the book we discussed the fact that the low barrier to entry business (usually the one that competes on price) will have no end of entrepreneurs, big companies, venture capitalists and investors having a go and winning market share. History tells us that we can make quick and accountable returns when at scale if competing on price. But, my friends, never forget it's difficult for a SME to make money when it competes on price. An entrepreneur chooses this business because they see it as achievable.

But then there's the rare breed of entrepreneur – the Walt Disney, the Steve Jobs – who would not dream of status quo in their entrepreneurial success. They believe in dreams and barrier breaking. The trouble is that after the initial 'Ohh' and 'Ahh' moments, over time that special something becomes more standard in the experience arena. The impossible has been made... well... possible. If you then compound that with success, you will create competition.

There will be people who love what you do and try to copy it, failing miserably. This is fantastic – I'll explain why shortly. Then there are those who see what you do and copy it at the same level, or even higher. These will be few, but they will be driven individuals, and this copying happens now at a faster rate than ever. News is spread quickly due to the net, unlike the months it took before. Any exploration into the unknown creates a buzz – it always will. With this buzz, especially in business, comes glorious interest and free publicity.

Your competitors start by being in awe of what you have done. Then they become jealous and want to muscle in to help themselves to some of your pie. It'll take longer for others to catch you up if you're smart and experience led – if you've built a high barrier to entry business, they will have those high barriers to climb. But some will climb them.

Before we look at what to do about the serious competition, let's look at the tryers who don't do the right thing. They want to copy you without the effort, and they may steal some custom at first, but they'll soon alienate these customers, turning them into fans of your experience business.

This is best explained in a recent story of mine.

A few years ago, Partyman launched a festival for children which we wanted to be really good. We called it KidsFest – I have always been a big fan of calling companies or businesses what they are. It saves so much time and effort on marketing, but on this occasion it came back to bite me. Another local business did the exact same thing, setting up its own Kids' Fest, and customers thought it was us.

Luckily, I have a name in my armoury that is unique – Partyman. It's taken sixteen years to build, but this time and effort has given me a trusted brand to use, the hallmark of the Experience Business. So naturally, I then called my festival 'Partyman's KidsFest'. We lost money for three years, but invested a ton of value so that by year five we would have a stable cash generator for the business – forever.

The copycat company tried to do what we did, but in a bid to turn a profit right from the word go, it charged far less and had no margin to invest into delivering a great experience. It was a disaster that made the national press, front page too. All this did was give us kudos. People were soon saying, 'Make sure you go to the KidsFest run by Partyman.'

So investing time in building your name is vitally important.

What about the other side of the coin – the ones who actually do things well, and better?

Walt Disney changed theme parks for ever. It's taken three or four decades for the rest of the world to catch up, but Universal has now raised the bar with the Wizarding World of Harry Potter.

Partyman's Christmas Experience is now not the only experience in the UK which has moved mountains. Competitors are moving mountains too, and if we don't move forward, we will no longer be the most amazing. We'll drop down to 'really good'.

Competition does positive things too. Firstly, it educates pioneer companies that there's a new standard. This turns their mind to accepting that they need to invest in staying ahead.

Coffee shops have created a conglomerate of experience-led shops together. Starbucks made the first move with high-end sofas and expensive lattes, then the Costas and Neros muscled in. Coffee shop competition helped Starbucks become a commoditised experience, and now many people will not accept instant coffee. They'd rather pay prices that twenty years ago they wouldn't have dreamt of paying.

Some of your organisations may become commoditised Experience Businesses. Embrace this – it is far better than a commoditised price-led business. Commoditised Experience Businesses are the ones that get the big money at exit. People will want to buy into you, or buy you out. You could even be the person who creates a new economy of experience – this is happening every day.

When the competition creeps up, stand your ground, build and be prepared to share a little knowledge. You'll make friends within your competition, which is a good thing as together you'll create the Experience Economy. Keeps raising the quality and offer of your experience and you'll stay in the lead. After all, you'll always be the original. The trick is to stay original.

CHAPTER 12

The Experience Business's Life Journey

I think it's important to understand the life journey of the Experience Business – the points of stress and cash burn; the dedication needed to get over the potholes. My summary here is an amalgamation of my educated thoughts, research and experience with my own companies. I have case studied multiple companies to show some patterns, including those that compete on price, and my general rule of thumb is that as a price business reaches its peak profits or goes bust, an experience business is just getting going.

Apple started in 1976, but the iPhone wasn't launched until 2007. Yes there was some cool stuff before, but the real money making and value came about then, thirty-one years later. Disney started in 1923, but kicked off serious profits thirty years later. Rolex was founded in 1907 – it's 110 years old at the time of writing.

So rather than put timelines in years, I think of them as stages. Every business goes through the same journey as it grows from startup to big business. I call this the Business Life Journey. I was inspired by Daniel Priestley who mapped the 'Entrepreneur Journey' in his book *Entrepreneur Revolution*. I have added my spin to his model by looking at cash flow and cash burn.

Cash flow usually ramps up in a price-led business faster than in the Experience Business. But those fast pounds don't stick around long. Cash burn is what can kill a company – the bigger you grow, the faster the cash burn. Sure, the scales tip eventually and you'll generate cash, but many don't survive the process of cash burn. Understanding it's going to happen to most businesses gives you the tools to navigate it.

If it does generate reserves, the business can self-finance and make more and more, but until that time, it's important for you to understand at what stage cash burn happens. This will help you navigate the storm.

Now let's look at the stages of the Experience Business.

Stage 1 – the vision. The Experience Business plans its vision from the outset, sharing with the world a story of the greatness it's about to unfold. This is powerful and promotes traction. It also attracts dream stoppers and mood hoovers who question the feasibility of the project. As with any business start-up, you need resilience here.

The Experience Business has a vision that states what it is. Compromise will never be accepted.

Stage 2 – price resistance. Building margin into the price of a product can result in people not wanting to do business with you. To survive Stage 2, consistently deliver the best experience to the people who use your business. Be aware that it will take some time to win round a mass customer base.

Stage 3 – a few love you. By now you'll have a number of advocates and some fans. These will advertise you via word of mouth, and more customers will come. The risk now is leveraging your fan base too soon or without proper funding.

Stage 4 – cash burn through growth. You start to grow. For example, maybe you go from owning one restaurant to owning two. Your quality is compromised, but you still have a fairly good brand. Then the business starts to discount and move away from its vision to survive cash burn. This puts out the fire, but as a result fans drop down to advocates, advocates become customers. You're on the journey to commoditisation.

Stage 4 – winning fans back. Three things can happen now. The business might shrink back to what it was originally, then slowly get its fans back, becoming an amazing lifestyle business that makes decent profits for its owners. Or it might go bust after a period of flitting between being price-led and experience-led. This is what usually happens.

The third thing that might happen is the business owner fights back and finds investment and cash to pursue their dream and scale an Experience Business. This is difficult – only 0.5% of start-ups manage it, but it's possible.

When a business survives like this, it gains fans and testimonials. People love its good works and something amazing starts to happen. Those who can't afford the prices the business charges wish they could, and in many cases find a way to do so.

Stage 5 – *recognition that you're the best*. Either at scale or lifestyle size, this stage puts you in the profit leagues. The business can re-invest in itself and customers fall more in love at every transaction. It's like a snowball of excellence.

At this stage, great people want to come and work for you. It's a win-win.

Stage 6 – *fans*. Forget shoppers, you now have predetermined customers ready to buy. They quickly become fans and attract more customers to the business.

Stage 7 – *scale the Experience Business*. Now the business is at the right stage to expand. Banks are willing to lend money, and in most cases enough cash has been built up in the business. Greatness can begin.

With scale comes...

Stage 8 – opportunity. If you choose to, you can now leverage your brand assets, either alone or with partners. Be careful whom you choose and how fast you diversify, though. Look for people aligned to your culture. You will even be able to become a commoditised business, selling standard stuff with a twist and pricing accordingly with a margin.

For example, John Lewis opened Waitrose, selling food with a higher margin than its rivals. But because people love the John Lewis brand – hey presto, they love Waitrose too.

Stage 9 – legacy. Last but not least, the business gains a legacy, and shoppers naturally become customers to businesses with legacy. Legacy gives the business a higher value.

CHAPTER 13

ExperiEnce Starts with Easy Peasy

So here's the thing: this book, and anything you commit to, must be backed up with evidence. You can argue with opinion, but it's impossible to argue with evidence. However, I hate what I'm going to share with you in this chapter.

I've discovered something that's at odds with my core beliefs about running a business. It's like someone showing you water running uphill. Every part of you says that it's not possible, but the evidence is staring you in the face.

Things evolve, I know that, but sometimes things change faster than we expect. I've always believed that good old-fashioned human interaction is a key part of every business operation. For years, I've heard people railing against robot phone systems: 'Press one for this, two for that, blah, blah'. People want to talk to real people, not robot voices.

At least, that's what I used to think.

But now, the simple truth is that more and more people *don't* want to interact with humans when they're doing business. They want to self-serve. They want to interact with a website, an app, a machine. The shift is happening. I've seen the evidence in my own businesses and it's a game-changer for us all.

I'll give you two real-life examples about how my own habits have changed. Number one – when the supermarkets introduced self-checkout lanes a few years ago, I said they were a silly idea because people liked talking to the checkout assistants.

Now I go straight to the self-checkouts.

Number two – up until recently, I booked all my international travel over the phone. I wanted to speak to a real person. This week I booked a flight to Hong Kong on the Virgin Atlantic website – no human interaction required.

Two small examples, but they are backed up by what Partyman customers say, which is generally that they prefer to self-serve instead of be served. Before long, some customers will want to do *everything* without interacting with a real person. So businesses must allow their customers to self-serve. Too many businesses still force human interaction.

I'll come on to more evidence later in this chapter, but first, let me talk about some of the ways this shift is going to impact businesses.

It's worth noting that humanising a business is expensive. That's why businesses want to do away with people. In all my companies, we have frequent discussions on how we can control our labour costs. Robots are taking on an increasing role in the workforce, to the point that Microsoft founder Bill Gates recently suggested that robots should pay income tax.

Business owners who fully understand this concept and integrate self-serve channels into their businesses will enjoy significant growth in the coming years. People will choose to do business with them at the expense of old-school competition.

Many business owners (including me) have been in denial about what customers actually want. Until I thought about it properly, I didn't fully understand what is happening. I was so convinced that a great human-delivered experience was what people wanted, I was blind to the reality. People are changing; technology is making them less and less patient. They moan like hell that the internet is slow, or if they lose reception on their phones so they can't put that photo on Facebook right now. Heaven forbid they have to call and book a table for dinner because the booking server has crashed on the restaurant's website.

Recently, I parked in a car park that didn't have a contactless card machine, forcing me to spend ten minutes sifting through my glove box looking for £3.60 to pay. That's ten minutes of my life I won't get back.

The result? I'll avoid that car park at all costs from now on and park in the more expensive car park that accepts card payments.

The evidence shows this is what people want. They're tech hungry – they want it faster, easier and *now*.

Most company chiefs, shareholders, and all business owners I speak to believe in great customer service. The trouble is, we may not understand what part of the service our customers want to be better. The evidence hasn't been presented correctly, and because we're living it, we may not realise the huge shift we're going through. My belief is that for menial and boring tasks, people want to do away with humans altogether. They want to self-serve.

Therefore, any time-save or task-save adds to the attraction when a consumer is deciding whether to do business with us.

I turn now to McDonalds. Did you know that the 'drive-thru' makes more sales than the restaurants? The appeal of not having to get out of the car saves time and drives sales. Guess what Starbucks and Costa have started doing? Drive-thrus, so people can get their sticky mitts on an espresso and cinnamon bun without taking their hands off the steering wheel. Furthermore, I've seen more self-serve coffee machines than ever before.

Experience creates loyalty, but I think we may be looking in the wrong places to create that loyalty.

As a business owner, and after speaking to thousands of business owners, I understand the two things businesses want:

to get customers and keep customers. At a higher level, they then want those customers to spend again and again. We call this the 'retention and repeat' rate. The change to self-serve is ongoing in every walk of life. We can even live in smart homes which deliver effortless living experiences – no longer do we need to turn the heating on manually; our home will do it for us.

Our companies need to be effortless experiences, too.

Let's look at a sector that twenty years ago I'd never have believed you wouldn't need a human to deliver the service: banking.

UK banks have seen, year-on-year, branch footfall decline. Customers now use either telephone banking or internet banking. It's easier and quicker, and 24/7. I can transfer money on my phone using my thumb print – an easier, more effortless experience than Julie in the bank trying to sell me something, or having to talk to the cashier through an inch of bulletproof glass.

At its heart, self-service is consistent. People want you to be easy to do business with. This is what creates loyalty. And the fastest way to drive customer loyalty is to deliver a positive first experience derived from speed, effortlessness and simplicity.

The fact is: we want to self serve because we know, deep down, most employees just don't deliver to the standards the owner or CEO thinks they do or the customer wants and desires.

I know it to be true. Even as I'm writing this, I'm still slightly in denial that my customers want it.

I'm wrestling with my core deep down. You see, I know that when I'm buying, I try to self serve before I switch to a human in so many daily tasks.

Switching is the little aggravation, like a flea that stops the customers cming back. Avoid it as much as possible.

Before we go on, I need to explain "'switching'" and "'services'".

Let's, for arguments sake, say a potential customer wants to do business with you. He or she can use all of the following to make contact with you:

- Email

- Social media message

- Website

- Web chat

- Call

- In store

- Self-serve in store

- Post.

If the customer chooses 'in store', they may then have to buy online because their desired item is out of stock. What they've had to do is switch services.

My companies believe in mitigating switching between our services. But I'm not happy with just that; I try hard to improve the ease of each service so it is the only one a customer needs to use.

The following exercise will give you some key pointers to improve your business's experience, and improve your sales as a result. Remember: people are becoming less patient – they want speed.

Ask yourself, 'How can I stop customers switching services?' and 'How can my business be more effortless for my customers?'

A simple survey is best for answering these questions. All of my companies have a call centre team. These guys talk to customers all day long – evidence and research lies here. Copy us: set up a survey. Then, when the phone rings, ask your customers questions which will help you understand if they switched from one service to another before they called to speak to a human.

The first question after the polite intro could be: 'Did you go on our website before you called us?'

You may well discover that a good chunk of your calls are only happening because another service didn't deliver. Usually the self-serve channel didn't allow the customer to do what they wanted to do, so they had to call up to solve the problem.

A classic (stupid) omission on my companies' self-serve channels was the postcode. Being businesses with destination venues, we had to make sure people knew how to travel to us, so they wanted our address for their satnav. But they couldn't find the postcode on our website. I mean, it was there, but you needed a PhD in postcode pursuit to find it. All our customers wanted was to know our postcode. But they couldn't find it on the website within 45 seconds, so they switched service and called us … but sometimes we were busy on the phones. So they emailed us. Then they messaged us on Facebook…

And so it goes on. Too many channel switches before the issue is resolved. Not good.

What did we do? As a simple remedy we placed the postcode under the phone number on our website, with the words: "SATNAV post code CM3 5WP" in addition, we put it in the top right hand corner.

This evidence proves that, with a little digging, we discovered overwhelming evidence that our customers had tried to self-serve first, but were forced to switch communication channels.

Imagine how many calls you could reduce pre-sale if customers self-served. Imagine what costs that would save. Then you could use that resource to improve your business and your customers' post-sale experience. A seamless self-service option allows you to reduce the cost of selling. And that's where this gets really exciting.

People want to buy online, and we get a lot of our sales during out-of-office hours. They want to communicate when it suits them. They may want to buy at three in the morning, and frankly, why not? If that's easier for them, it improves their experience of doing business with our company. This is why it's imperative our 24/7 services get as much (and arguably more) attention than the phone or in store services. We're investing a considerable amount of money in self-serve to improve our switch rate, but there are things you can do without spending money.

In many cases, companies use a language people don't understand, or build a service that doesn't help customers answer their needs or solve their pain. Customers just want the solution to be easy and effortless. If it isn't, they'll promptly switch to human-led services. And be annoyed.

Think of yourself as a newbie shopper, looking to use your business for the first time. Kick off with your website and look for the nasties listed below:

Language. Have you made it easy for people to understand what they need to do? Complicated terminology and jargon force people to switch service for clarification.

Null search results. Websites which have search bars are a regular let down. If customers can't immediately find what they're looking for, they'll either go elsewhere or switch services.

A simple web tool will allow you to see what people are searching for. In many cases, they are using slightly different words which mean the same thing.

Too much information. Reams of text put people off. They don't want to read it. Bullet points, spacing between text, headings and videos will help.

The price. The classic of all classics – believing that Price On Application is the way to go. It's effort, and deters customers. They want to know the price *now*.

Our research

Getting your customers to self-serve isn't the problem. Chances are that they'll be doing it in droves already, and the tide will turn further. The big challenge we've found in my companies is to create an effortless self-serve environment that doesn't force our customers to switch channels to complete their goal.

The results are in, people, and they're not what we anticipated. What percentage of our callers were channel-switchers, only calling because they couldn't do what they wanted to do via self-serve channels?

Ten percent? Twenty? Nope, try half.

A full 50% of our callers were channel-switchers. If we could help them to self-serve, then our incoming call volume would drop by half, and we'd have happier customers, and more of them, too. A proper win-win.

Obviously, there are reasons why companies are putting off introducing self-service. Investment may, in many cases, mean a chunky upfront cost. But the argument for it should not be 'It's nice to have' but 'It's an essential to have'. And it will become more and more so as time trundles on.

Small stores may not be able to afford the fancy self-service tills popping up in large supermarkets now, and they may argue that they're different, but where are the shoppers going? They're going to the big stores where it's easier to park, easier to shop and easier to pay. Effortless.

Obviously a bank of twenty self-serve tills would have been a significant capital expenditure, but very quickly the big store will save that on salary cost, and they'll win more sales from customers who prefer to self-serve

Eventually the investment will pay back handsomely, and it'll be the same in most businesses. Here's what I predict will happen. The real winners from self-serve will be the businesses who which take the front end savings from their de-humanised selling process, and invest that money in the backend. The businesses which reduce their costs on the frontend and wow their customers on the backend will create more loyalty and build an Experience Business. It's at the backend stage people want companies to surprise and delight them. They want a great waiter who is passionate and loves his or her job and takes the time to tell them what's on the menu, but they want it be effortless to book the table and get to the restaurant. The person who used to be on the phones can now be used to market the business instead of dealing with the business niggles.

Phew... I'm saved. We're all saved. There is a reason for our existence after all.

People want to buy easily and effortlessly. Most companies will see self-serve as cost saving which will catapult the bottom line. Far smarter to take half the saving and invest it back into creating a better customer experience.

CHAPTER 14

Thirty-five Awkward Questions

You have probably been giving some thought as you've read through this book to the differences between businesses which compete on price and those that compete on experience. I'm guessing you'll know which camp you sit in. Perhaps you are thinking about ways that you can improve the customer experience in your own business, creating fantastic, memorable, sharable 'wow' moments that will attract customers, keep them, drive up spend and create raving fans.

Before I pull down the curtains on this book though, I've got one more chapter I need to share with you, all about how you can turn the concept of an experience business into a reality.

Understanding the benefits of customer experience is all well and good, but it's got no value until you translate it into the real world. Now I need to share with you how you can turn the concept of an Experience Business into a reality. One percent inspiration and ninety-nine percent perspiration is the truth. You need to be the catalyst for change in your own business.

In this chapter, I'm going to share thirty-five questions that I ask of my own businesses to create effortlessness, ease of use and memorable experiences. The task ahead of you is not an easy one. Building a super-systemised business that hits ten out of ten on every customer satisfaction score is never easy. I know that we're some way off it in my own businesses, but we're working hard every day, striving for continual improvement. The bigger the ship, the longer it takes to change course, but the magic is in making a start. And that's exactly what I hope these questions will help you to do.

1. *Is it easy to buy from you?* Ease helps to create loyal customers. We've all dealt with companies which make us phone up in office hours, and leave us on hold for long enough to grow a decent beard. We've all dealt with businesses which need the order faxed to them. And I'm sure we'd all rather use Amazon one-click.

Ask how you can reduce friction, reduce the number of clicks, do away with barriers and hoops and make it easier and faster for people to buy from you than from anyone else.

2. *Is your business self-serve ready?* A growing number of people do everything they need to do without interacting with another human. McDonalds has worked out that the key to faster fast food is getting rid of human interaction.

Self-serve is faster and more consistent than humans, and customers can use it in the middle of the night.

To become an Experience Business, ask how you could give customers the chance to self-serve as well as a 'done for you' option.

3. How can you stamp out negative language? The process of moving negative language to positive is a massive plus. It's what we do naturally in our lives – kids are very good at it. In our personal relationships, we use positive language to play down a negative.

If, for example, your partner asks, 'Have you put the bins out?' you're not likely to respond with a flat no. You're more likely to reply with something positive, like, 'I was just about to' or 'It's the next thing on my list'.

Positive language is a small change with a big impact, and it can have a huge impact on customer experience.

A client calls to find out where her delivery is. The typical response would be something like 'It won't be dispatched until tomorrow. You'll get an email', which is hugely negative. The exact same message can be delivered as 'Good news! It looks like it's going to be dispatched tomorrow, and we'll email as soon as it's on the way to you'.

A tiny movement to positive language can be fantastic at making customers feel great.

4. *When can you ask for feedback (and act on it)?* Building a feedback loop into your business can be one of the fastest ways to improve your customer experience. Sounds obvious, but too few businesses do it.

Once the customer has transacted (whether that's buying something or coming to an event or whatever), send them a message asking them for feedback. Here's the exact email I've sent out a couple of times to gather feedback from customers, and it works really well:

> Thanks for coming to our live event on Tuesday, it was great to see you. I'd love to know what you thought. I'd really value your feedback on the following two questions. What went well? What could we improve next time? If there's anything else I need to know, don't hold back. Thanks in advance, James.

Asking for feedback is only half of the job, though. If you invite feedback, then you're in dialogue with your customer, so thank them for their input, show that you appreciate what they've said, and explain either how and when you're going to implement their recommendation or why you're not going to.

Customers love to see continuous improvement, especially if they're regulars to your business. Invite them to drive the change and you're pulling them closer to you, making them feel valued and dramatically improving their experience.

5. Can you reduce backend friction in your business? Even businesses which have reduced friction on the frontend and made it easy for people to buy still have friction on the backend, which destroys customer experience.

Take online clothes shopping as an example. It's so easy to order clothes online now, but I rarely do because I know that if they're the wrong size, I'm never going to bother to send them back. It's just too much hassle to box them up and get to a post office.

Some companies have overcome this with prepaid return stickers and collections directly from their customers – all good stuff that reduces friction after the sale and encourages loyalty.

When you make the return and refund experience fantastic, you'll hugely improve your chances of getting repeat orders from customers because you will have reduced the fear of buying from you.

6. Can you speed up internal processes? People want instant – instant pain relief. Instant problem solving. Instant answers. Nobody wants to wait for an age any more; people haven't got the patience. When things go wrong, your customers want a speedy conclusion. The last thing everyone needs is a problem festering.

If you can't instantly give the solution the customer is looking for, but you will deliver a solution eventually, ask yourself what's stopping you from speeding the process up. Don't be the company that slows things down for customers due to some stupid rule or other. That's not a good experience; it winds people up, amplifies their pain, and will have a huge negative impact on their loyalty.

7. Can you pre-empt your customers' next move? Train your company to pre-empt the next move not just when things go wrong, but to wow customers when they go right by making the next move even better.

Hiring a car is a classic. When people hire a car they have to find the darn thing, work out how to open the boot, and then figure out how to take the handbrake off. Making sure the car is easy to find and giving your customers the information they need to get started is a simple win. You know they're probably going to ask the questions, so why force them to wait?

Think, what's the next thing your customer will need? How can you add value by providing it seamlessly?

8. How can you give your customer more than they expect? Businesses have a terrible tendency to oversell and under deliver – we used to do it in some of my companies. The fashionable approach for businesses seems to be to load on as much as possible to the product or service, make it look desirable and sell it. It might create more first-time sales, but from an experience perspective, all this strategy does is dramatically increase the chance that your new customer will be disappointed with what you've delivered.

The smarter way to play the game is to hold something back. Don't list every single benefit when you're selling, and then surprise your customer with something that they're not expecting. You'll need to create margin in your service to do this consistently, and it does make it harder to get first time sales, but the referrals, testimonials and repeat sales you'd expect from an Experience Business will be much easier to get.

9. How does your body language translate? Body language is a secret power in customer service. If people look slouchy and unmotivated, that automatically triggers in the back of the customer's mind the idea that the product or service is slouchy.

Promote happy, confident, welcoming body language. It drives people to come and engage with your team and your company.

10. What does your tone convey? Tonality is the secret power cousin of body language. It's often overlooked in a business capacity, but used naturally in our personal lives the world over. Watch a child quickly master it as he or she coaxes their parents to allow them to do what they wish.

How can you help your team to remember that the way you say it is more important than what you say?

11. Do you know whom to call Sir and whom to call Dave? I learned in my early career that there's a real skill in knowing how to address your customers. Too many businesses are way too formal in their approach, calling everyone Mr and Mrs, or Sir and Madam.

In my businesses, we try to maintain a friendly image rather than a formal one, so our default is to use people's first names where we can – that's what works for us. People like hearing their own name, so using first names and a friendly approach drives loyalty. A quick win, and one that seems to be growing in popularity is businesses asking permission to use a customer's first name. I like this approach – you'd be hard pressed not to feel slightly more at ease when someone asks permission to use your name. It's so simple.

12. Are you building a happy and hardworking team? It's long been a policy of mine to recruit on attitude over skillset. 'Happy and hardworking' are the primary traits I wish to see represented in my team.

Happy people are naturally spreaders of happiness. It's contagious; their happiness will rub off on people and create a good feeling. Only happy people can drive positive experiences. As humans, we're reactive to our environments, but we're more reactive to the people in those environments.

Get people with the right attitude and skill them up your way – it's a smart approach, very rewarding, and in many cases cheaper than recruiting skilled people while you're growing. But reward your loyal staff when you get there.

13. Are you still doing the basics? Companies love to try fancy new approaches to improve customer service. As the years trundle on by, I have come to realise more and more that the basics always win.

I love the simple stuff like clean uniforms and smartly presented team members; I love hearing the phone answered in a professional and welcoming way, and experienced staff using a bit of common sense to help customers.

You're not overlooking some of the basics, are you?

14. Do you keep your promises? It's easy to make promises, much more difficult to keep them. Failing to make good on your promises is what loses customers, though.

Promises happen without us even knowing it. Brands create a promise with every sale. The first time we buy from someone and the service is good, they have made the promise that the second time we buy will be exactly the same. At least, that's what a customer naturally thinks – it's why we have our favourite brands. The promise of consistency for ever.

If you make an obvious promise, make sure this too is kept. Breaking promises erodes trust and loses customers quickly.

15. Have you forgotten the power of a smile? A warm look and a welcoming smile go a long way. We know it, but we forget it, focusing instead on the hard aspects of customer service.

Remind and train your team to deliver friendly eyes and happy smiles.

16. *Are you too slow to say sorry?* Stuff goes wrong, and it always will. No matter how hard you try, you're still going to have problems. Finding a resolution for them is one of your biggest wins from an experience perspective. It starts with an apology.

Too many businesses don't say sorry, and that's a mistake.

I find that raving fans are often born out of mistakes and problems. When you apologise (and mean it) then strive to put things right, customers become customers for life.

At Partyman, we have become experts in saying sorry. We bend over backwards to make amends for a problem, and the result is an army of massively loyal fans.

17. *Is information about your values freely available?* Research buyers are not a trend in decline. But it's not just prospective buyers who'll look you up before they buy. Increasingly, great people who are considering working for you will check you out first.

People like to feel good about the businesses that they buy from, supply, and work for. Articulate your company values and allow people to find them easily. It is just another little win when it comes to driving experience.

18. Do you change for the sake of change? Companies change on a whim. How frustrating is it when you go to a restaurant to find it's removed your favourite dish? The chef got bored, so he changed the menu, but he works there five days a week, and you only go in once a month.

'Entrepreneurs' boredom' is exactly the same. Too many business owners get bored of whatever they're doing – even if it's working really well. They focus on the new rather than the successful. I've been guilty of this, too many times.

Make sure you have a democracy of management that will debate and squash quick, stupid changes.

Asking customers and surveying them leads to wins in decision making for change, but never be the fool who listens to the loudest. In most cases, the silent majority are the ones who will hate the changes. Invest in ways to learn what the quiet customers want.

19. Are you prepared to change? Change for the sake of it is a bad thing for customer experience, but any business that let's grass grow under its feet is likely to wither away in time. So don't avoid change completely – you must be prepared to adapt and evolve.

Established business leaders like a steady approach, but there will always be a fresh-faced entrepreneur looking to shake things up and lure your customers away. Think Kodak, Nokia and Blackberry – businesses that didn't evolve, didn't embrace change when they needed to, and paid the price.

My approach is to offer my ideas and new thinking to my team in the hope that they may run with one. The balance between my entrepreneurial desire for change and theirs for consistent management means we generally reach a happy medium of organic change rather than a wilting death.

Knowing when to change and when not to is a tricky conundrum for any business. Keep it under constant review and do everything you can to understand your customers.

20. Do you act like a credible expert? Working with tons of business owners, I've learned a few things about how they promote themselves. There are those who never look the part, but they're actually experts and really good at what they do. There are the novices who act like experts. They look the part, win market share, but when the marketing and hype disappears, customers often feel let down and resentful. Then there are the experts who act like experts. The book cover looks good, and the story is good too.

Most businesses sit in the first camp – they're too modest to blow their own trumpets. The real goal is to be in the third camp – be an expert and convey that fact to others. Get that right and instead of you chasing customers, they'll flow towards you.

21. Do you treat customers like your grandma? I admit, this isn't my phrase. It's something that Disney coined, but I believe that it's bang on for explaining the customer service dream for excellence. If you can treat every customer like they're your grandma, you'll win.

For the most part, people have a tendency to be lovely to their elders. They give up seats for them, are warm to them, use perfect tonality and body language, show ultimate respect. These are the building blocks of great service and fantastic customer experience.

22. Are you progressively improving? Companies need to strive for continuous improvement. It doesn't matter if the improvements are only minor – it's the mentality behind the improvements that matters most. Improving things tells your customers and team that they are involved in a progressive company that they can be proud of.

23. Do you ask customers what they want? Asking customers what they want and for feedback, you will drive a sense of ownership in your company through them. This is a real 'winner, winner, chicken dinner' moment.

I regularly talk to customers, ask for their opinion, and when necessary tell them why what they want isn't possible, but what I could do as an alternative. This creates advocates who stick up for my businesses. I am open to opinion, and freely give mine.

Listening to customers will make them feel fantastic.

24. Are you consistent? Consistency makes a brand. It sounds so simple, but it's not.

The bigger your business gets, the more difficult it is to maintain consistency, but that's how a powerful brand is built. And that's how prospects and customers will come to know what to expect if and when they interact with you.

Consistency feeds through into the language you use. Would one of your customers know that an email was from your business just from the way it was written?

25. Are you stealing your customers' time? This question is as valid online as it is offline. If you've got wait times and queues then you're stealing time from people. Destroy those time stealers and you'll give your customers the most precious gift of all.

Giving time drives experience above all else.

26. Do you inform customers of troubles ahead of time? Telling customers about trouble ahead of time can often dampen frustration. If possible, offer a solution or alternative.

Imagine you find out that your flight is delayed by four hours when you're standing at the gate. There's little to do, no place to go. You're likely to be frustrated. But if you'd been informed the previous day, you could have changed your plans and built your schedule around the new take off time.

The more warning you can give of problems, the less frustration they'll cause.

27. Do you anticipate what your customer will want next? As things change in a fast-paced world, make sure your company meets those changes ahead of time. Simple things like having a website that works on all devices or allowing your customers to contact customer support using Facebook messenger, Slack or even WhatsApp.

Only a decade ago many companies didn't have a website, and still some businesses insist on fax correspondence. It's almost laughable, but that's what destroys customer experience.

28. Do you shock and awe? Leave people in awe of your experience. Shock them with moments that seem free and unbelievable. In effect, give them more than the marketing tells them and more than they feel they have paid for (as long as margin allows).

29. Do you say thank you? Once the sale is in the bag and the customer is at home on their sofa, that's the time to say thank you. Get the timing right and thank sincerely, and you'll drive experience and loyalty. A handwritten card goes a long way here; it's a lovely, personal touch.

30. Do you show up when customers least expect it? My Bank manager Peter Quinn sent me some flowers on the birth of my son. I didn't expect that – I have told the story countless times, he checked in with me as a client when I least expected it and I'll never forget it.

31. Do you offer a guarantee? Companies that publicly and easily offer money back guarantees and no quibble refunds get brand loyalty and trust in one go. This is especially important for first transactions, but even repeat customers will be comforted by a solid guarantee with no small print.

32. Does your team look the part? It's scientifically proven that teams and companies that use names on uniforms or in offices promote a better experience. I love being able to address new starters by their name, and customers love it, too. People feel relaxed when we use names – this drives relationships.

If name badges are not a viable option, make sure you introduce yourself to customers. This will have a massive effect on rapport.

I am so passionate about great looking uniforms and name badges for our business, I know when I see smart attire and positive-looking team members I feel good about the business. This is a simple win – smiling and presentable people do make great first impressions – do your team fit the bill?

33. Can you make your customers 'famous'? For some companies it's possible to elevate customers within the tribe and make them famous. Football clubs allowing kids to lead the players out will create a new generation of loyal fans. Ask customers to be featured in a newsletter or video, or on your website or social media. It will help to pull them closer to you and feel great.

34. Can you make your staff 'famous'? You can't weave experience into your business without having your team onboard, and sometimes a great way of rewarding staff is to make them famous within your world. Shine a light on them, whether it's with an award or interview. Share the news internally and in customer communications. Hold them up as an example of great practice. They'll feel good about it, and others will follow.

35. Do you tell your story? Companies that weave stories through their DNA promote better team productivity and create raving fans. Customers like to feel they understand the journey that got you to success.

SUMMARY
Building Your Legacy

We're coming to the end of our time together, so I want to summarise my vision for this book. I've learned that sustainable customer experience and service can only come from a company that has meat on the bone. The system, the profit and a grasp of numbers are all foundations of an excellent company.

I have run enough businesses to know you need a set of rules and time investment to allow you to achieve excellence constantly and consistently. Great service that delivers experience can only come from a company that charges the right amount with the right margins. Experience companies need big margins and big profits to deliver the experience.

The big, big money lies in either building a huge 'price' company like McDonald's, or an excellent experience company like Apple or Disney. Many of you reading this book will be running an SME, not even touching the empires of the above businesses, but it's possible to build an excellent big *small* company that competes on experience. You will then be the emperor or empress of your Experience Business. You'll be testimonial famous, inundated with fans and loyal followers, then you'll be able to increase prices over time. You'll master continual profit creation easily when your customers are predetermined to buy from you, whatever you sell.

The great news is you now know how to be small but profitable in your niche – if you compete on experience, you'll be able to scale the business up at your leisure.

The experience business is a legacy business. It takes longer to build than a price-led business, but stays around for longer too. It is born from consistency of system and a powerful vision from a driven entrepreneur who loves what he or she does, in turn getting a team behind the story. The loyalty, effort and dedication from this amazing team creates customers who then become fans in love with the business. This builds a legacy that can last centuries.

Coutts, Rolex, Harrods, Savile Row, Ferrari, Rolls Royce, Disney will be around 100 years from now.

To your continued success...

THE AUTHOR

James Sinclair is the founder and CEO of the Partyman Group and the founder of Success Seminars.

James started entertaining as Jimbo the Partyman at the age of 16, slowly building up an entertainment agency and then, through a combination of acquisition and organic growth, moved into soft play venues, childcare and laser arenas.

The Partyman Group generates sales of over £12m a year with a team of 350, working across multi locations in London and the South East, including a 70 acre Farm attraction in Essex.

James has won prestigious business awards including 'Young Entrepreneur of the Year', 'Growing Business of the Year' and many more.

With his entertainment background, James is one of the UK's most popular business speakers and that demand was fuelled by the publication of his first book 'The Millionaire Clown' in 2015.

James is available for speaking engagements by contacting www.jamessinclair.net.

Based on his entrepreneurial experiences James launched Success Seminars to teach, support and inspire business owners on their entrepreneurial journey. Information about the seminars and live events can be found at www.jamessinclair.net.

James lives with his fiancée Natalie and son Harvey in Essex. As well as being CEO of The Partyman Group, writing books, speaking across Europe and running his seminars, he documents his entrepreneurial life on his video show 'Backstage Business'.

Follow James and keep learning at:
www.jamessinclaire.net
www.backstagebusimess.co.uk
www.partyman.co.uk